THE COMPLETE
PRESENTATION
SKILLS
HANDBOOK

How to Understand and Reach
Your Audience for Maximum
Impact and Success

SUZY SIDDONS

KOGAN
PAGE

D1019178

London and Philadelphia

First published in Great Britain and the United States in 2008 by Kogan Page Limited

120 Pentonville Road
London N1 9JN
United Kingdom

525 South 4th Street, #241
Philadelphia PA 19147
USA

www.kogan-page.co.uk

© Suzy Siddons, 2008

ISBN 978 0 7494 5037 3

British Library Cataloguing-in-Publication Data

A CIP record for this book is available from the British Library.

Library of Congress Cataloging-in-Publication Data

Siddons, Suzy.
   The complete presentation skills handbook / Suzy Siddons.
         p. cm.
   Includes bibliographical references.
   ISBN 978-0-7494-5037-3
1. Public speaking. I. Title.
   PN4129.15.S56 2008
   808.5'1--dc22

                                                            2007044005

Typeset by Saxon Graphics, Derby
Printed and bound in India by Replika Press Pvt Ltd

Contents

Acknowledgements   *vii*

Introduction   **1**

1. **Why Give a Presentation At All?**   **5**
    Are presentations worth the effort?   5
    Benefits of a successful presentation   7

2. **Setting Expectations**   **11**
    The delegate's kit   12
    Booking venues   15
    Greeting the delegates   16

3. **Researching Your Audience**   **20**

4. **Audience Behaviours**   **25**
    Learning preferences   25
    Aiming   28
    Encoding   31
    Transmission   32
    Receiving   33
    Decoding   34
    Responding   34

5. **How People Remember, What They Forget**   **38**
    The four stages of memory   38
    Associations and differences   41
    Numerical information   43
    Primacy and recency effect   45

6.	**Selecting Your Subject and Organizing Your Information**	**47**
	Setting SMART objectives	48
	Organization methods	51
7.	**Writing the Script**	**54**
	Structuring a script	55
	Scriptwriting rules	58
	Style and vocabulary	60
8.	**Visuals**	**65**
	Brightness and afterimage	65
	Layout, templates and typefaces	69
	Using presentation software to the full: the power of hyperlinks	70
	How to prepare a hyperlinked show	72
	Adapting information for slide shows	74
9.	**Staging the Presentation**	**76**
	Space	76
	The presentation area	79
	Lecterns	80
	Lighting	80
	Acoustics	81
	Optional extras	81
10.	**Voice and Performance Skills**	**82**
	The voice itself	86
	Does my accent matter?	96
11.	**Nerves and Body Language**	**98**
	Charisma, authority and influence	100
	Use of space	101
	Learning to observe	101
	Proxemics	103
	Displacement activities	104
	Creating rapport	105
	Spot the liar	105
	Putting body language together	106
12.	**Using Microphones and Autocues**	**107**
	What you need to know before you use a microphone	107
	Types of microphone and how to use them	109
	Autocues	111

13.	**Rehearsals**	**113**
14.	**Equipment and Visuals**	**120**
	Clicker / Wireless Pocket Presenter / Presentation Remote	120
	USB flash drive	121
	Image banks	121
	Presentation checklist	121
	After the presentation	124
15.	**The Question-and-Answer Session**	**126**
	Preparing for the question-and-answer session	127
	Types of questions to expect	130
	Tracking the question-and-answer session	133
16.	**Delivering the Presentation**	**135**
	First impressions	135
	Credibility – what the audience believes	135
	The charisma recipe	137
	Starting with a bang	138
	Your final bow	140
17.	**Technical Presentations and Demonstrations**	**141**
	Technical presentations	141
	Setting demonstration objectives	144
	Demonstrations	147
	The sales cycle	151
18.	**Controlling the Audience**	**155**
	Handling interruptions	157
19.	**Handling the Media**	**158**
	Just before an interview – taking control	162
	Preparing for an interview – the five-step preparation process	163
	Getting help before an interview	163
	The actual interview	166
	Handling discussions	167
	Other hints and tips	169
20.	**Training People to Give Presentations**	**170**
	Training yourself	170
	Training others	173

21. **The Role of the Master of Ceremonies**   177
    The MC's duties before the presentation   177
    The opening welcome and introduction   179

22. **Following Up the Presentation**   183

23. **Alternatives to Presentations**   186
    Successful meetings   186
    Tasks necessary for any meetings   187
    Attendees' checklist for meetings   190
    Leader's checklist   191
    Attendees' personal checklist   191
    Organizer's checklist   192
    Teleconferencing and video conferencing   192

24. **Handling Disasters**   194

Appendix: Templates, Checklists and Reminders   *196*
    Master checklist   196
    Personal profile   198
    Self-assessment   199
    Feedback sheets   200
    Delegate kit   204
    Evaluation form   205
    Sample course questionnaire   206
    Rehearsal checklist   207
    Templates   210
    Hints and tips on preparing presentations   217
    Flip chart questions and answers   219

Index   *221*

Acknowledgements

I would like to thank Samantha Warner for her invaluable help with the information about the latest technology in Chapter 14.

My thanks also to the staff at Reflex Limited, who have for years provided me with information about projectors and screens.

Also, heartfelt thanks to my husband David Nickson, without whom...

Introduction

This book is for anyone who has to give a presentation of any sort to any kind of audience. Never let presentations or public speaking worry you or your company again. Here's the complete solution. Whether it's presenting your company internally or externally, giving good or bad news, selling, persuading, training or handling the media, this compendium of skills covers sound working practices, exercises, checklists and case studies to make sure that organizing and giving presentations and public speaking of any kind becomes a pleasure and not a burden.

Each section will contain: an introduction to the subject; background information on the subject; best practice; hints and tips; step-by-step guides; case studies and exercises where appropriate. Sample documents, slide and handout formats are in a separate appendix, as is a list of useful publications.

The three essential ingredients of a presentation

The audience

Why are they there? What do they want from the presentation? How do they listen? What will they remember? What will turn them on or off, make them comfortable or uncomfortable? What language do they speak? How much do they know? What questions will they ask? What will they find hard to listen to? What are their business needs? How do you find out about them? Can you analyse their response? What might make them hostile? How will you get feedback from them?

You – the presenter

Why are you there? What do you want to achieve? What do you look like, what do you sound like? What will you do about nerves? How will you rehearse? How will you remember what to say? What is charisma? How will you handle questions? What will you do if they are hostile? How will you keep your energy up? If you are being interviewed, how will you handle this? Do you need a Chairman or Master of Ceremonies? How will you introduce yourself? Is there an efficient way of handling the technology?

The presentation itself

What is it trying to achieve? What is it about? What are its limits? What visuals or handouts will be needed, what technology is available? How long should it be? Will it need following up? How will the information it contains be remembered? Which parts will be difficult or hard to under-stand? How will the script be prepared? What about the location and staging?

Each of these three ingredients is vital to a successful presentation – like a three-legged stool, when all the legs are there it is stable, but remove or shorten one of them and the whole thing collapses. No matter how well-constructed the presentation is, if it is badly delivered it will fail; no matter how well-delivered the presentation is, if it doesn't make sense then it will fail. Most importantly of all, even if the presentation is perfect and the presenter inspired and charismatic, if the audience isn't interested or engaged, then the presentation will certainly fail.

All these factors and many more will be covered in this book. By the end you will have a tool kit for success, and presenting will never be the same.

Before you read on, here is a questionnaire about how you feel you perform when presenting. Bear this in mind as you read on.

Self-assessment

Look at the categories below and give yourself a score to show how good you consider your skills to be in each area.

Table 0.1 Self-assessment: structure of the presentation

	Good	Fair	Poor	Oh dear!
Organization				
Logic				
Interest to the audience				
Presentation of benefits				
Positive start				
Powerful ending				
Good, concrete examples				
Length				
Balance between theory and reality				

Table 0.2 Self-assessment: stance and posture

	Good	Fair	Poor	Oh dear!
Confidence				
Gestures				
Eye contact with the audience				
Personal appearance				
Use of the presentation area				

Table 0.3 Self-assessment: visual aids

	Good	Fair	Poor	Oh dear!
Clarity				
Interest				
Number of slides				
Added value				
Equipment handling				

1

Why Give a Presentation At All?

'Presentation' is a very inexact term – it covers everything from your first job interview to a retirement speech, from a standard sales pitch to a health and safety lecture, a progress report to a project team to an appearance before a tribunal – anything that involves speaking to an audience of more than one or two. So why do we do it – is there a compelling business reason for one person to spend the time and effort to put a presentation together – and more importantly why a group of busy business people should sit and listen to that person?

Presentations are an extremely expensive way of getting your message across. Well-paid and high earning sales personnel may be worth at the very least £1 per minute. Imagine then, an audience of 20 salespeople, listening to a half-hour presentation. This is £600 worth of time. If you then add up all the time that they spend listening to presentations (often up to four hours per week) you get to the massive figure of just over £9,000 per year per person. This is £9,000 worth of time that they could have spent selling. Add this to the amount of time that is spent preparing, delivering and following up presentations, we are looking at a very significant sum indeed.

Are presentations worth the effort?

It may seem strange to begin a book on presentation skills by questioning the very need for presentations at all. This, however, is something that is not done rigorously enough. All too often we deliver presentations without thinking through the genuine benefits that this particular method of passing information to others should bring, let alone concerning ourselves with what the audience wants to gain from the presentation.

Table 1.1   Good and poor reasons for giving a demonstration

GOOD REASONS	POOR REASONS
• If you need to communicate time-critical information to a large group of people	• Because we always have presentations on Thursdays
• If you need to persuade an audience to make a choice, change their mind, take a set of actions or pass on information to others, and you need to do it *in person*	• If the information you are giving is already known to the audience and the presentation neither re-interprets it or puts it into a new context
• If the audience is interested, concerned or needs to hear what you are going to say	• If the audience isn't interested in what you are going to say, or doesn't need to hear it.
• If you need to teach skills or give information cost effectively to more than three or four people at once	• If the *audience* doesn't know why they are there, or *you're* not sure why *you* are presenting
• If you have a clear set of objectives for the presentation	• If you have no objectives for the presentation
• If attending the presentation will act as a bonding exercise for the people involved	• If the audience feel they have better things to do
• If you have the time, energy and commitment to make the presentation	• If you are in any way half hearted about the presentation

There are several major factors to consider before you start to spend any time on preparing a presentation. Ask yourself the following questions:

■   Is there a better way of getting this information across? Could I use e-mail, a written report, a short meeting, a conference call or another method?

■   Have I got all the information I need?

■   How much will this presentation cost and is it cost-effective?

■   What is this presentation for? What will the audience do, think and feel after they have heard the presentation?

If the answers are 'yes', 'no', 'too much' and 'no idea' then you should seriously consider whether a presentation is the best method in the first place. If you think about all the presentations you have sat through in your career, I wonder if anyone could honestly say that every one of them was worth the time and effort involved?

A good presentation contains many of the same constituents as a good book. The readers should be curious about the subject. The writer should be at least literate, if not magnificent. The chapter list should be interesting and understandable. The words should be the best possible. The appearance of the book should be impeccable. The reader should have somewhere to sit and read comfortably. The typeface should be easy to read, and it is helpful to know where and when they can find the book in the first place.

The most important factor in the success of both a book and a presentation is the attitude of the consumers. Just as you cannot force people to read something they neither like nor need, so you should never force-feed an audience with indigestible, unnecessary, uninteresting or irrelevant information. The audience's attitudes, responses, reactions and needs throughout the presentation are of paramount importance – in fact, without an audience you have no presentation.

So is there a perfect recipe for a presentation? Can a presenter realistically expect to please all the audience all the time? Of course not. What an effective presenter can expect to do is to put the message across in a way that involves the audience both intrinsically (by making them react, think, and compare) and extrinsically (by making them discuss, find out more or take certain courses of action). An effective presenter can also expect to leave each member of the audience feeling that they have learned something that is of use to them, in a way that made the information real to them personally and with a clear sense of what the next step will be.

Of course, the presenter cannot do this without knowing a considerable amount about the people who are going to be in the audience.

Benefits of a successful presentation

When people listen to presentations, they hope they will hear things that will do some of the following:

Table 1.2　What a presentation should achieve for the audience

- Make money or save money
- Save time or effort
- Make them comfortable
- Improve their health
- Save them pain
- Make them popular, famous
- Attract the opposite sex
- Help them to take advantage of opportunities
- Help them to be unique
- Help them to protect their reputation
- Help them to gain control
- Keep them safe
- Gain them praise
- Conserve their possessions
- Increase their enjoyment
- Satisfy their curiosity

- Protect their family/business
- Make them stylish
- Satisfy their appetites
- Allow them to copy others
- Give them beautiful things
- Give them good ideas
- Give them an expert vocabulary
- Help them to take advantage of opportunities

- Help them to choose between options
- Confirm their expertise
- Solve problems for them
- Amuse them
- Give them am inside view
- Confirm their decisions
- Open new markets for them
- Help them to avoid criticism
- Help them to avoid trouble

If what you are going to say doesn't do any of these – don't say it.

Here's an example of a pointless presentation. The presentation was given every half-hour to small groups of possible buyers at a huge motor show by the chief engineer of Vitessimissimo Motors, a very prestigious manufacturer known for high-quality, high-performance sports cars. The car itself was slowly rotating on the display stand along with a lissome lady and a great number of brochures. The stand was also fully staffed with salespeople with a large screen at one side showing a looped video of the car speeding along roads in the Tuscan hills. The brochures contained the following information with very good photographs of the car.

The presenter had 10 slides, each of which contained the information in one of the rows of the specification and nothing more. The presentation took about five minutes, after which the sales force moved among the audience to answer any questions. The presenter was a brilliant engineer, but sadly, not the world's greatest speaker. His script consisted of reading every word on each slide ... slowly. When asked why he was giving the presenta-

Table 1.3 Specifications of the Vitessimissimo Gran Turismo

Engine type	4244cc, eight cylinders
Power/Torque	399bhp / 7100rpm / 339lb ft / 4750 rpm
Transmission	Six speed automatic
Performance	0–62mph: 5.2sec / Top speed: 177mph
Fuel/CO_2	19.2mpg (combined cycle) / 345g/km
Price	£84,500
Gearbox	Conventional automatic transmission
Included	Satellite navigation system, 4 cup-holders
Date of release	October

tion he told us: 'All the other stands have live presentations, so we thought we should as well.'

Now here's an example of where a presentation was really needed:

The venue is a central London Hotel. The conference is for directors of building companies in the south-east, some of whom (but not all) belong to the SE Builder's Association. Next month, legislation is proposed to ensure that any building projects in flood plains, brownfield sites or green belt land follow a set of new and extremely complicated criteria. The speaker is the chairman of the SE Builder's Association who has been closely involved in the drafting of this new legislation. His association runs an extremely useful interactive website that has highlighted three major concerns and shown that there is much confusion about exactly how this legislation will affect planning permissions. He intends to:

■ give a general overview of the new legislation with advice about where to find out more about it;
■ address the three major concerns;
■ discuss the impact of this legislation on building costs, time scales and logistics;
■ take questions.

His objectives are:

■ to clear up any misunderstandings;
■ to gain new members in the association;
■ to get feedback on any parts of the legislation that are unacceptable to his members.

Not only has he his own set of objectives, he has also asked the attendees (via the website) what they want to hear about, and has set his agenda accordingly. There is every possibility that his presentation will be useful, extremely interesting to the audience and therefore successful.

Exercise

Scenario: a medium sized retail store has one department selling small electrical goods (irons, toasters, mixers, coffee machines, electric carving knives and so on). A manufacturer's rep wants to come and give a presentation to show the new products that his company is producing. The department has an electrical buyer, two assistants and a storekeeper who are all frantically busy.

Is a presentation the best way to get the (simple) information about the new products across? What else could be done?

Exercise

Scenario: an insurance company is changing the cost of their policies significantly. This is partly due to changes in the law and partly due to the rising claims caused by what appears to be climate change. Undoubtedly these changes are going to make the policies harder to sell, and there are legal and financial implications that are complicated and hard to understand.

The sales force is in the dark about this and naturally worried. Is a presentation to the sales force called for? What else could be done to get this information across quickly and effectively?

As with every consideration in this book, the audience's needs are paramount and even the slightest suspicion that you might be wasting the audience's time should give you pause for thought before going to all the effort required (on both sides) for a presentation.

Summary

The three ingredients for a successful presentation are the audience, the content of the presentation itself and the presenter – of these, the starting point should always be the audience. If you consider their needs and interests, you can't go wrong.

2

Setting Expectations

When does the presentation begin? When you step onto the stage and start to speak? Or is there anything you can do to predispose the audience to listen actively and positively?

There is indeed a great deal that you can do to set the audience at ease. For those of you who are used to organizing and giving presentations these considerations will seem like self evident truths, but as with most things, the devil is in the detail and the sheer scale of logistics for a presentation can often scupper the project before the audience even arrives.

Take this scenario. You are a wheelchair-bound consultant at a major London hospital. You have been asked (by your boss) to attend a conference at the London headquarters of a major drug manufacturer. You have never visited these headquarters. The presentation he wants you to attend is at 10 am on Monday 13 October. Your field of interest is rheumatology. You know that this manufacturer has developed a drug that can successfully treat arthritis. What else do you need to know?

Let's start with the basics:

- What is the address exactly?
- Whereabouts in the building will the presentation take place?
- Does your enterprise have a contact there?
- What is their phone number and e-mail address?
- How can you get there and how long will it take?
- What about parking?
- What about disabled access?
- How long will the presentation last?
- Will there be time for questions?
- Are there any other presentations taking place with this one?
- Is there an agenda?

- ■ Who else will be attending?
- ■ What is the presentation about – exactly?
- ■ Who will be speaking and what are their credentials?
- ■ What will you gain from this presentation?
- ■ Will lunch and refreshments be provided and is there a vegetarian option?

If you don't get answers to all these questions, you will be uncomfortable and unprepared, and therefore not positively in favour of attending. What you really need is for the people organizing the presentation to send you a delegate's kit.

The delegate's kit

Table 2.1   A sample delegate's kit

Page A: Title page
Conference Title: Living with Arthritis
Sponsored by: The Arthritis Trust and Jollydrugs Plc.
Location: Conference Room 1, 3rd Floor West.
Address: Jollydrugs House, 14 Ashbourne Way, Notting Hill, London W8 XXX.
Date: Monday 13 October 2008.
Duration: 9.00 am–4.30 pm.
Contact: Maria Grey, Tel: (020) 7222 444 Email: mariag@jollydrugs.co.uk.

Page B: Location map and directions page
(Include a location map here.)

BY ROAD
Southbound motorway exit beyond Junction 13 OR Northbound motorway exit at junction 15
Take the A2111 to Notting Hill and turn into Ashbourne Way. Jollydrugs House is the tall building opposite the police station.

BY RAIL
Take a train to Paddington Station;
Take the Underground to Notting Hill;
Turn left at the station, second right and Ashbourne Way is on your right. It is a three minute walk from Notting Hill station.

BUSES
27, 27a, 204, 311

BY TAXI
Taxis available at Paddington Station.

PARKING
There is a large reserved parking area and easy level access to Jollydrugs House.
Disabled parking is provided for 10 cars.

BY AIR
London Heathrow

Meeting rooms: There is a lift to the main conference room and a wheelchair lift to all other meeting rooms.

Dining room and coffee lounge. Both of these rooms are on the ground floor with excellent access and our dining room tables have been adapted to be wheelchair friendly. There is always a vegetarian option available at meals.

Hearing aid loops: There is a hearing aid loop in the conference room.

Page C: Programme Page

TIME	EVENT	SPEAKER
8.45 am	Registration and coffee	
9.00 am	Welcome	Dr Maria Grey
		Chief of Research
		Jollydrugs Plc
9.10 am	Introduction	Professor Jack Ketch
	Diagnosing the problem	Managing Director
		The Arthritis Trust
10.00 am	Presentation	Dr Phillippa Brain
	'Miraclextra, the drug of	Chief Research Chemist
	the future'	Jollydrugs Plc
10.50 am	Coffee	Etc.
Etc.	Etc.	

There will be time for questions at the end of each presentation. Handouts will be provided.

Page D: Delegate list page

Delegate name	**Company**
Dr Betty Ford	Glaxcombe Plc.
...	...

Page E: Biography pages

Dr Phillippa Brain
As Chief Research Chemist of Jollydrugs Plc, Dr Brain has been working for seven years with her team on the development of Miraclextra. Her sectors of research also include tracking the side effects of arthritis drugs in general and specific work on ...
    Papers published include: 'Arthritis and Ageing ...'
    Her presentation 'Miraclextra, the drug of the future' will cover the development and testing of the new drug. Results so far, acceptable side effects and contraindications ...
At the end of the presentation, delegates will be fully up-to-date with the latest research in this field.

Page F: Presentation page

(List the slides that will be used in the presentations.)

Page G: Evaluation form: general

The Arthritis Trust would be grateful if you would take a few minutes to complete this form and hand it in at the end of the conference.

How useful do you think this conference has been?

Not at all					Very
1	2	3	4	5	6

How did you rate the quality of the conference?

Poor					Excellent
1	2	3	4	5	6

Do you feel that the conference will be of use to your company?

No					Yes
1	2	3	4	5	6

Page H: Speaker evaluation
Speaker name:

Was motivated and enthusiastic about the topic	1	2	3	4	5
Presented the material in an informative manner	1	2	3	4	5

Any other comments:
Speaker name:

Was motivated and enthusiastic about the topic	1	2	3	4	5
Presented the material in an informative manner	1	2	3	4	5

Any other comments:

Page I: Conference environment evaluation

Administration	1	2	3	4	5	6
Refreshments	1	2	3	4	5	6
Venue	1	2	3	4	5	6

What I found most useful from the conference: _____

What I found least useful from the conference: _____

Please give any other comments that you feel would help us to improve conferences in the future.

_____

Pages F, G, H and I can be given out at the actual presentation.

A carefully prepared delegate's kit will allay any pre-attendance concerns that the attendees may have and should predispose them to think positively about what they are going to listen to. There are other things that help with this too:

▓ name tags for the delegates and speakers;

▓ name plates for the speakers on the platform;

▓ a seating plan (if appropriate);

▓ water and mints;

▓ seating plans for lunch;

▓ clear signage for the conference room, coffee break room, rest rooms and restaurant;

▓ paper and pens for each delegate.

Never underestimate the importance of making the logistics of any presentation as clear as possible. If the audience doesn't feel that their needs have been considered they may well have a negative mindset before the presenter has even started speaking.

Booking venues

The other side of the coin is how the organizer goes about setting up a presentation. Here are the things that you need to think about when organizing a conference or set of presentations at an external venue. The same criteria also apply when you are giving a presentation in-house.

▓ What are the charges or cost per delegate? Where can you get information on prices and / or an estimate?

▓ How well equipped are the conference rooms? You will need a range of equipment. Decide what you need for the venue to set up your room as required. Ask to see a full equipment list.

▓ What are the settings like in the conference rooms? The conference room should be laid out in an appropriate style – theatre, classroom, board room, café, etc.

▓ Is it possible to have a working lunch? Is advance notice necessary?

▓ What capacity is the conference room?

▓ Where is the conference room located? Do they have a location map?

▓ What are the parking facilities? How far is the venue from public transport?

▓ What kind of food is on offer? Are special diets also available?

▓ Is secretarial help provided? Are there any facilities for those with disabilities?

▓ What facilities are there for the organizer? Will they provide you with a welcome desk, phone line and computer/internet modem line? Will there be a manned reception desk and how will people register?

▓ Do mobile phones work in the venue?

▓ Can they provide overnight rooms for the conference organizer and the first speakers?

Greeting the delegates

There is a comforting ritual that happens when people greet each other. It's a natural pattern – we do it almost instinctively and it clearly signals that we are pleased to see our visitors and that we welcome them. It's our way of easing the passage between arriving as a 'stranger', i.e. someone invited onto another person's ground, to feeling included in what is going to happen there.

If done well, it is the start of a successful relationship because it makes our visitors feel special. If done badly or left out it makes the 'stranger' uncomfortable and often hostile.

This is how it goes: there are seven stages to the ritual.

▓ Stage 1 – The invitation and Stage 2 – the directions
These should be as personal as possible. The initial invitation should be addressed to the visitor, by name. A letter, a warm email or a telephone call will do it. Now this can be difficult if you have a huge audience of which you know only a few people, but still, a personal letter and a delegate pack that covers everything will do the trick.

▓ Stage 3 – The 'inconvenience display'
This is the amount of effort that you, the host, make when you are welcoming the visitor. This does not mean that you have to welcome each visitor personally (although for very important visitors you should make the effort). It is to do with how easily visitors can identify where they are supposed to be and whom they are supposed to meet. Good signage helps here, as does having enough people to cope with the rush of arrivals at the start of the presentation sessions.

The length of time you keep people waiting without any information can have a significant impact. One to five minutes' waiting doesn't upset people; five to fifteen minutes' waiting may make the visitor worried. 'Have I come to the right place? Have I got the date and time right? Are they expecting me?', are the thoughts that will be going through their heads. Fifteen to 20 minutes' waiting may well lead to hostility and 20 to 30 minutes to extreme hostility. 'If I've made the effort, so should they, I'm just as important as they are, they're inefficient and I don't like this, if this is the best they can do, why should I trust the speakers …' are common responses.

Over 30 minutes' waiting is appalling – if they haven't left by that time, they will almost certainly wish they had, and this is not the state of mind you want the audience to have. Keeping people informed about what is happening helps the situation but you, as organizer, need to ensure that there are enough people around the reception area to make this unnecessary. It does not make sense to have one overburdened receptionist for a conference of 200 people.

It is important to start the conference on time – just as the audience doesn't want to wait to register, they don't want to wait for the speakers to start. This brings us on to the problem of latecomers. This is inevitable as traffic and transport become more congested. Latecomers obviously want to be there and are usually flustered and frustrated with their journey. Make sure that even though the conference or presentations may have started that there is still someone there to greet them, and that there are seats at the back of the presentation room for them to sneak into and sit.

■ Stage 4 – The 'distant display'
These are the things we do naturally when we see someone we are expecting. We smile, tilt our heads slightly, raise our eyebrows and often make a gesture towards the visitor. So no matter how busy the 'greeters' are, take the time to really look at the visitor and meet them with a smile.

■ Stage 5 – The 'close display'
This is where we actually come into physical contact with our visitors with a handshake. This is usually the only time in business that we actually touch people. A handshake gives a great deal of information about ourselves to the person we are greeting – and vice versa:

- The 'wet lettuce' handshake. Limp, damp and unconvincing, no muscle tone, no grip and absolutely no enthusiasm shown for the person you are greeting. While concert pianists, and micro surgeons and the Royal Family need to protect their hands, most of the rest of us don't.
- The 'lobster grip' handshake. A pincer movement where the hand is held like a lobster claw and the visitor's fingers are nipped between the thumb and other fingers. This is very cursory and not at all friendly.
- The 'iron glove' handshake. This is intended to show strength of character, dominance and general control. It is a particularly forceful, gripping handshake and often hurts, particularly if you are wearing rings on your right hand.

- The 'get down, Fido' handshake. Another dominant handshake where the shaker grips the shakee's hand and turns it over so that their own hand is on top.
- The 'politician' handshake. This is intended to be warm, caring and intimate. The shaker clasps the visitor's hand lovingly, bringing the left hand up to also clasp the visitor's forearm. Can be misconstrued and feel over-familiar.
- The 'I hope you have no diseases' handshake. Here the shaker briskly shakes hands and almost immediately withdraws their hand as if touching might convey some appalling disease. Not friendly.
- The 'straight from the shoulder' handshake. Very manly this, the shaker keeps their arm really straight, thus forcing a distance between them and the visitor. Supposed to be straightforward and manly, but not very warm.

So what is a really effective handshake? There are these ingredients: speed, clasp, length of shake and eye contact. Take your time with a handshake, reach toward the visitor with a smile and place your hand into the visitor's hand as deeply as possible, the web of skin between your fingers and thumb should come into contact with the web of skin between their thumb and fingers. Your fingers should curl round the rest of the visitor's hand firmly but not too hard. Shake fairly slowly while smiling and maintaining eye contact. Withdraw your hand slowly.

Exercise: Handshaking

Over the next few days, shake hands with as many people as possible. How do you respond to their handshakes? If you have a group of friends, you might like to give and get feedback on your handshaking styles.

■ Stage 6 – The 'grooming display'

This is basically the 'small talk' session where you get comfortable with each other (talking about the weather, the journey and so on). Don't miss this out – getting down to business immediately may save time, but it doesn't put you – or them – at ease! This is basically what the coffee session before the presentations is designed for: it gives visitors the time to get used to their surroundings and the people there.

▥ Stage 7 – The farewell.

This is basically a reverse of the last three stages. Small talk, the farewell handshake, best wishes for the journey and so on. It is very important visitors should be escorted out.

Summary

Never underestimate the importance of getting the logistics right for the attendees, make it as easy as possible for them to get to the venue, register and get comfortable. Knowing what to expect from the presentation and the presenter primes them to listen.

For smaller audiences you can set and check expectations more personally. Try to call or e-mail the attendees beforehand and find out what they are interested in, what they already know and what they are concerned about. The next chapter looks at how to analyse the audience before you meet them.

3

Researching Your Audience

The more you know about your audience, the more relevant and interesting your presentation will be. Not knowing your audience is lethal. How can you engage people, if you don't have a clue what really interests them? But how can you find out? Where do you start?

Recently I was at a small conference on a small island. There were seven speakers in all and we were talking about various aspects of how companies could develop their staff and improve their motivation and company commitment. None of the speakers had ever met anyone in the audience before – the only people in the room that we knew were the conference organizers and a director of the institute sponsoring it. I had had about two months to prepare the presentation – so where to start?

First and foremost I knew that whoever came was interested in developing their staff – they were not forced to be there, so I could assume that the subject was important to them. Next, I knew that they all belonged to the same institute so could assume that they were possibly from the same field in business (in this case, human resources). Finally, I knew that the majority of the audience came from the same island so their general business, economic and social concerns would perhaps be similar.

Already then, I knew where to start to research: the island's business community, institute's concerns and interests and recent developments and thinking about human resources (and of course the specific subject that I had been asked to present).

Finding sources of information was easy – the Island Tourist Board and Chamber of Commerce provided an excellent overview of the business community. The institute's website and brochures were a good source of current thinking about employee development and changes in human resource practices.

Next came the individuals in the audience. We were all sent a list of the people attending, their job titles and the companies they worked for. When this was analysed the results were: 40 people in human resources, two members of the press, eight from support services such as the ambulance service, education, health and social services, five managing directors/CEOs and a handful of students. There were also four people from a well-known optical services group and another group of five from one particular bank. Well over half of the audience worked in the banking sector.

Now it was possible to dig deeper. Websites, professional bodies and trade journals provided in-depth information on what had been happening in the various fields of business, and colleagues who had had dealings with some of the individual companies gave feedback and advice.

For the next few weeks the financial pages and appointments sections of the press became favoured reading and every item of radio and TV news became a source of information. Finally I visited a branch (local to me) of the optical services company and a branch of the bank with five attendees and told them what I was going to present, and they filled me in on their interests and concerns.

Exercise

You have been asked to speak to an audience of 25 from your local Women's Institute about a trip to France you recently made. You are a member of the same WI and live in the same town. What assumptions can you make and how will you research the audience in more depth?

Exercise

You have been asked to speak to a group of dealers who sell your company's products about the new products that your company will supply next year. What assumptions might be dangerous and how will you research this?

Exercise

You have been asked to give a presentation to an investment bank that you hope will invest vast amounts of money in your start-up company. You cannot afford to make any assumptions whatsoever. How will you go about researching your audience?

Having analysed the whole audience and researched its background, you now need to find out as much as you can about the individuals in your audience. Obviously with a large audience (over 50) it would be difficult to research every member, so you need to pick a representative few. In the case of the conference I chose two bankers, one of the opticians, two HR specialists and one person from education services. I prepared a little questionnaire …

- What particularly interests you about xxx?
- What experience do you have of xxx?
- What problems have you had with xxx?
- Have you had a great success with xxx?
- Do you have any questions you want to ask?

… and rang them up. As always I was delighted by the response – in the main I got through and people were willing to talk. This also meant that when I met the audience just before the presentation there were several people that I had already talked to, which helped with my nerves enormously (it's always a very good ploy to know at least two of the people in the audience – apart from helping with nerves, it also gives you someone who will give you feedback after the presentation).

There will also be times when you make a presentation to people you know well. Life is a great deal easier in this case because you can email them or speak to them directly or over the phone and find out exactly what they want and need to hear.

Exercise

You are about to lead a Project Team update meeting. You know all the individuals in the audience. Prepare a little questionnaire that you could use before you prepare your presentation.

Exercise

Your boss has asked you to give a presentation on the progress your team has made over the past month. What questions do you need to ask her before you prepare your presentation?

Exercise

You are going to an interview for a new job in three weeks' time. The interviewer is about to ring you to make the appointment. You know that you will need to make a presentation as part of the interview. What questions would you ask the interviewer that would help you to prepare an effective presentation?

Having researched the audience's workplace, background, business needs, concerns and interests, is there anything else you need to know?

Here's a cautionary tale. A colleague gave a presentation to a group of 20 dealers who sold the products his company manufactured. He was a technical ace and had carefully researched the dealers' levels of knowledge, areas of business, customers and sales records. He was presenting a very sophisticated and potentially profitable new computer that would revolutionize the market. It was a competent and effective presentation. At the end there was a strange silence in the room. 'Any questions?' he asked – and from the back came the sarcastic voice of the main dealer. 'Tell us about your delivery schedules ...'.

What had happened was that the last piece of equipment that he had presented to them had had serious problems with delivery, and the dealers were made to wait several months before the new kit was shipped to them. This had seriously affected their cash flow – so no matter how wonderful the new offering was, until they had reassurance that deliveries would be timely they were simply not going to buy.

Being a technical guru, my colleague did not know (and had not thought to ask) if there was anything in the trading history between the dealers and the manufacturer that might affect the presentation. The moral of this tale is that you also need to research the history of the relationship between yourself, your company and the audience, and bear this in mind before you put your presentation together.

Here is another cautionary tale. A friend of mine was asked to present to a high-powered group of personal assistants. The presentation (on office management and databases) was about to start when she happened to look out of the window and saw a steady stream of salespeople and staff getting into their cars and driving off. In fact the car park was emptying rapidly. When she commented on this she was told that the company was (as they spoke) going broke and people were being laid off. She asked how this would affect the people in the room. They didn't know but were obviously worried. She asked them if they would be more interested in hearing a presentation about how to be successful at job interviews. They would, and this is what they were given. Problem solved!

To summarize: The more you know about your audience the better. There are many, many sources of information – trade journals, company websites, professional societies, professional publications, news stories, colleagues, friends and, of course the individuals in the audience themselves. All the information you gather will help you to tailor your presentation to their needs. Don't be blinkered by your own field of expertise – you need as full a background as possible, and remember that events in the outside world will also influence the success of your presentation. There would have been little point, for example, in making a presentation on the benefits of a washing powder on the day World War Two broke out.

4

Audience Behaviours

Now that you have looked at the audience's needs in terms of business content, interest and concerns about the subject, we turn to the audience's personalities and thinking processes. This chapter looks at how people take in information, what influences the way they listen and how communication really works.

What are your favourite television programmes? If you were going to a lecture, what would you be interested in hearing? If you had to learn something new, how would you go about it? How did you learn things at school, university or in your job? These factors influence the way you will listen or learn at a presentation of any sort. They will also influence the way you give a presentation. So there you are – standing in front of twenty people, only some of which you know. How can you possibly please them all?

Learning preferences

The questionnaire in Table 4.1 will help you to understand how you respond to new information and therefore how you are likely to behave as a presenter.

Read through each set of questions and put a tick in the columns A, B or C if you feel you agree. You may well find that you agree with more than one choice.

Interpreting the results

It is highly likely that there will be more than one answer for each question (very few people have only one way of acquiring knowledge), so think hard about your preferences. If no pattern emerges (i.e. there is a fairly even spread of As, Bs and Cs) then you would be comfortable with any of the methodologies mentioned here. However, if a pattern emerges then look at the descriptions below, which give you an idea of the most comfortable ways of learning for As, Bs and Cs.

Table 4.1 Learning preferences

Set 1. Leisure pursuits	A	B	C
How do you like to spend your leisure time?	Reading/listening to music/TV/radio	Physical activities	Group activities
Set 2. Learning simple tasks (things like learning to use household equipment, using new tools etc.)			
How did you approach the task?	Made a plan and read the manual	Went ahead with no planning	Asked for advice
What did you use to help yourself?	Reading matter or reference matter	Trial and error	Found an expert
How did you consolidate your learning?	Scheduled regular practice sessions	Improved by doing	Asked someone to test them or check what they had done
How did you refine those skills?	Set incremental goals	Just kept on doing	Discussed progress with others
Set 3. Hobbies and pastimes (like sports, music, model making, collecting)			
How do you find out more about the hobby or pastime?	Books, reference matter	By doing it	Clubs, friends
How often do you spend time on your hobby?	Regularly	Spasmodically	When there's a meeting
Have you taken any courses or qualifications in the hobby or pastime?	Yes or intend to	No	Not unless the group wants to
Set 4. Business skills (MBA, professional qualifications, IT skills, handling new equipment/procedures, etc.)			
Why did you learn the new skill?	Part of a personal plan	It just happened	Peer pressure or the need to keep up with the group
How did you learn it?	By yourself or from reference material	By doing it	By asking others, having a mentor, discussion
How did you refine or develop the new skill?	Practice, reading/research	By doing it	Help from friends

A-type learners like to research things well, have a clear pattern to the learning process, like to do things step by step, are happy with reference material and are self-motivated. They need reassurance that they are reaching the required standards, so watch over them! They often have very high personal standards and can be highly critical of themselves. They are often not happy with experimentation or sink-or-swim situations and have a cautious and sometimes timid approach to new skills. They have a long attention span and often get completely immersed in what they are doing. They are happiest when working and researching alone, and while this can be very effective, it does not give them the chance to discuss and so refine their new knowledge.

B-type learners like to get on with things, they want to do it for themselves and usually have the confidence to try! They are not happy learning from the printed page or screen. You will need to keep a weather eye out for them in case they get into bad habits, since they usually find their own way of doing things (which may or may not be according to laid down procedures!) They become easily bored with repetitive tasks and activities that take a long time to give a payback. When in doubt they often guess the answer rather than refer to a manual or ask for help. They like working with others and can be easily distracted by others or tasks that seem more exciting. They learn fast and usually effectively but will often try to bend the rules to get a faster result.

C-type learners learn best when they can talk about what is happening and watch how others do things. They may be comfortable with learning alone, but they definitely need to discuss and clarify before they can refine their skills. They think holistically and like to know how everything fits together and what the background is to any new information. They're usually logical and will question anything that seems arbitrary or sloppily expressed. They are often intellectually experimental and will try to find other ways of performing or integrating tasks.

Table 4.2 Types of information that each listener likes

A	B	C
• Likes lots of facts	• Dislikes too many facts	• Likes background information
• Likes hard information	• Likes anything up to date and groundbreaking	• Weighs information carefully
• Needs time to think about what they have heard	• Likes to try for themselves	• Needs to discuss
• Likes handouts and details	• Doesn't read handouts unless they personally involve him/her	• Easily sidetracked
• Needs proof, reference sites	• Likes to know what other people think	• Needs to know the thinking behind information
• Likes guarantees	• Easily bored	• Ethical and logical
• Likes tried and tested results	• Likes attention	• Asks complicated questions
• Likes listening	• Not a diligent listener	• Hates humbug
• Will probably take notes	• Usually the first to ask questions	• Speaks thoughtfully and authoritatively
• Slow to ask questions	• Enthusiastic, speaks quickly, expressively	• Good listener
• Sceptical about extravagant claims	• Likes vivid language	• Likes experimenting and trying other ways to make things work
• Speaks slowly, carefully and often with a questioning inflection at the end of sentences	• Prefers images to numbers and dry facts	

Table 4.2 continued

A	B	C
• Stubborn, will not change easily • Relates facts to business issues • Not a lot of eye contact	• High eye contact • Likes change • Likes to lead • Relates facts to personal experiences	• Is concerned about how the information will affect people • Prepared to change • Takes an overall view • High eye contact

Now let's apply this to your audience. Just as presenters have their own ways of presenting, so audiences have their own ways of listening.

As you can see from the above, sticking to just one style of presenting will not help the people in the audience with different styles to be as comfortable as they should be. Even though the information being presented is useful to them all, the way in which it is presented makes a significant difference.

Exercise

You have been asked to give a presentation on a state of the art new car that your company has just developed. You need to cover the following subjects: design, performance, marque, safety features, models and options, futures, maintenance, warranties, distribution, reliability and compliance with green standards. Obviously the people in the audience (all directors of potential distributors) need all of the above information.

Thinking about the characteristics of the A, B and C listeners, which subjects are likely to interest each of them? Draw up a prioritized list for each type. Now take a look at all the advertisements for cars that you can find, on television and in magazines, and see who they are aimed at and who they miss out.

Now let's take a look at the stages of effective communication, as shown in Fig 4.1.

Aiming

This is what we do before we start to communicate. We think, feel, consider, decide and plan what we are going to say. It is an entirely internal process and is *completely invisible and inaudible to the receivers*. It goes on privately

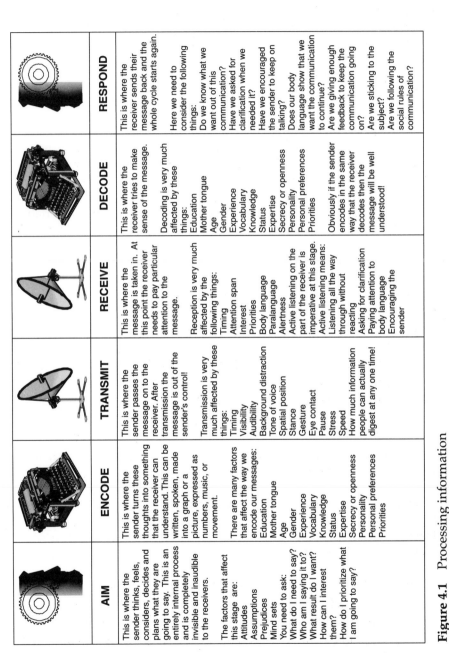

AIM	ENCODE	TRANSMIT	RECEIVE	DECODE	RESPOND
This is where the sender thinks, feels, considers, decides and plans what they are going to say. This is an entirely internal process and is completely invisible and inaudible to the receivers.	This is where the sender turns these thoughts into something that the receiver can understand. This can be written, spoken, made into a graph or a picture, expressed as numbers, music, or movement.	This is where the sender passes the message on to the receiver. After transmission the message is out of the sender's control!	This is where the message is taken in. At this point the receiver needs to pay particular attention to the message.	This is where the receiver tries to make sense of the message.	This is where the receiver sends their message back and the whole cycle starts again.
The factors that affect this stage are:	There are many factors that affect the way we encode our messages:	Transmission is very much affected by these things:	Reception is very much affected by the following things:	Decoding is very much affected by these things:	Here we need to consider the following things:
Attitudes	Education	Timing	Timing	Education	Do we know what we want out of this communication?
Assumptions	Mother tongue	Visibility	Attention span	Mother tongue	Have we asked for clarification when we needed it?
Prejudices	Age	Audibility	Interest	Age	Have we encouraged the sender to keep on talking?
Mind sets	Gender	Background distraction	Priorities	Gender	Does our body language show that we want the communication to continue?
You need to ask:	Experience	Tone of voice	Body language	Experience	Are we giving enough feedback to keep the communication going on?
What do I need to say?	Vocabulary	Spatial position	Paralanguage	Vocabulary	Are we sticking to the subject?
Who am I saying it to?	Knowledge	Stance	Alertness	Knowledge	Are we following the social rules of communication?
What result do I want?	Status	Gesture	Active listening on the part of the receiver is imperative at this stage.	Status	
How can I interest them?	Expertise	Eye contact	Active listening means:	Expertise	
How do I prioritize what I am going to say?	Secrecy or openness	Pause	Listening all the way through without reacting	Secrecy or openness	
	Personality	Stress	Asking for clarification	Personality	
	Personal preferences	Speed	Paying attention to body language	Personal preferences	
	Priorities	How much information people can actually digest at any one time!	Encouraging the sender	Priorities	
				Obviously if the sender encodes in the same way that the receiver decodes then the message will be well understood!	

Figure 4.1 Processing information

inside our heads and at great speed. Assumptions – attitudes, mind-sets and prejudices – are the factors that affect this stage.

These are the (not always logical) bases of what we believe. In presentation terms these may mean things like:

- 'They know more than me.' (How do you know?)
- 'They're highly technical, they won't want to hear about sales messages.' (Why not – they buy things too.)
- 'They'll know that already.' (A deadly one this – the more you know, the more you tend to think that others know. This is not always true – what might be a self-evident truth to you may be absolutely new and revelatory to others.)
- 'This will be too technical for them, they're salespeople.' (Another deadly assumption – they may not know the jargon but they will probably understand if you phrase it cleverly and without tech-speak.)

Assumptions should always be examined and checked – if you don't know the level of your audience's knowledge or experience, then ask them. Mind-sets and prejudices also need to be examined carefully:

- 'It will take me at least an hour to explain this.' (Think smart: less is more.)
- 'I'm breaking new ground here.' (How do you know?)
- 'It's an all-male audience, they'll never listen to a woman.' (Oh, come on – women do have the vote after all!)
- 'It's an all-female audience, they won't want to hear about technical details.' (See above.)
- 'I'll never remember everything I want to say.' (Make efficient speaker's notes, then.)

Our internal thoughts need to be examined as rigorously as the words we are going to use.

Having cleared your mind of negatives and preconceptions you now need to ask the following:

- What exactly do I need to say? What is the subject? What are its limits?
- Who am I saying it to? What do they do for a living, how can I interest them; and what sort of people are they? (As, Bs and Cs, for sure);
- What result do I want? What is the purpose of saying this? What's in it for them?

Now, how do I prioritize what I am going to say? Keep the Bs interested, involve the Cs in your thinking and give enough detail for the As.

All this may sound a very lengthy process – after all, you haven't even opened your mouth yet! And yet we do it every single time we talk face-to-face with anyone. We just need to be more efficient when we're talking to an audience.

Encoding

This is where the sender turns these thoughts into something that the receiver can understand. This can be written, spoken, made into a graph or a picture, expressed as numbers, music or movement. Think about this scenario.

Your four-year-old child has just asked you why washing up liquid makes bubbles. Would you give him or her a dissertation on the relative properties of alkaline substances and their interaction with water and air, or would you simply tell him or her that the washing up liquid traps air like tiny balloons? We automatically encode what we say to children because we know that they don't have the experience we have had that would allow them to understand a sophisticated explanation.

These are the factors that affect the way we encode our messages:

■ Education, experience and expertise – there is absolutely no point in giving highly specialized information that you have gained over a period of intense study, in a highly specialized way, to people who, for example have never studied beyond GCSE level. Trim your information to suit the educational and experiential level of the audience.

■ Mother tongue and vocabulary – unless you are lucky enough to be bilingual, you will need to slow down and simplify your language if the audience doesn't speak your natural language.

■ Age – I used to use the death of President Kennedy as an example of how highly-charged events are remembered – until I noticed the looks of blank incomprehension on the faces of most of the audiences, who hadn't even been born when Kennedy was assassinated.

■ Gender – even if men are from Mars and women are from Venus, it makes sense to use examples and references that include both sexes.

■ Status and secrecy or openness – this is a tricky one. We do tend to be deferential to those in very high positions – I often wonder if the unvarnished truth is ever presented to autocratic leaders. It's your call, but be aware that your encoding may well be altered if you are affected by the status of people in the audience.

▓ Personality, personal preferences and priorities – you need to make a few assumptions based on the general ways that people behave and encode your presentation accordingly, not just according to your own preferences. (See above.)

These are the behaviours you need to think about.

How fast do they like to act? Some people hate to be hurried when they hear new information – it takes a while for them to react, and they need to think about what they have heard before they decide whether the information is important to them. Conversely, some people are much more impetuous and will rush headlong into judgement about what they have heard, liking information to be presented to them quickly and with charisma. How can you, the presenter, cater for both of these needs – for surely, you will have people of both types in the audience?

Start with a positive attack, this will keep the impetuous happy, and follow up with hard facts and reference sites, as this will keep the As and Cs on track.

How much detail do they want to hear? If you need to go into great detail, then put the information into a handout. The As will be happy, the Bs probably won't read it anyway and the Cs will read it later.

Transmission

This is where the sender passes the message on to the receiver. After transmission the message is out of the sender's control! Transmission is very much affected by these things:

▓ Timing – when is the presentation taking place? Prime times are in the morning, but not just before lunch, in the afternoon but not just after lunch and not just before the close of the day. The three 'non-prime' times are unavoidable, but since the audience is either thinking about eating, thinking about digesting or thinking about going home, when you get these slots you need to be aware of the clock and the dangers of over-running, particularly at the close of the day. No one will be listening to your immortal words if they are thinking about traffic jams on the ring road or train timetables.

▓ Audibility, pause, stress and speed, tone of voice – if you can't be heard, you won't be understood. To make sense of what the presenter is saying the audience needs all the clues available to make meaning clear.

▓ Visibility, spatial position, stance, gesture and eye contact – if you can't be seen, your message is harder to understand. Radio is a marvellous medium, but you will notice that successful speakers have well modulated voices. Equally when the presenter is visible they have a barrage of aids to understanding at their disposal, where and how they stand, what gestures they make and possibly most importantly whether they make eye contact with the audience. Low eye contact equals low credibility.

■ Background distraction – if this is within your control, the audience should not be distracted by external traffic of any sort and this definitely includes mobile phones.

To end this section on transmission, it is important to remember that any audience is restricted by the amount of information that they can physically process at any one time. Cognitive overload (more than six or seven facts at any one time) exhausts them and leads to irritability and forgetfulness. Break your information into digestible chunks.

Receiving

This is where the message is taken in. At this point the receivers (the audience) need to pay particular attention to the message. Reception is very much affected by the following:

■ Timing – not just the time of day, but whether the individuals in the audience perceive they have the time to listen to the presentation. Research on the part of the presenter will uncover people who have other calls on their time and need to leave early – if this is the case, get your important messages across in the first parts of the presentation and leave the detailed explanations until last.

■ Attention span – individual attention spans vary widely. As seem to be able to concentrate for considerable time spans whereas Bs have short attention spans and need to be regularly re-engaged to keep them listening. Cs listen well but do need to discuss.

■ Interest and priorities – for really important presentations it is useful to do a survey to see what they are really interested in and what their priorities are, and then order the presentation accordingly.

■ Body language – how can you tell when people are listening carefully? There are several indicators – they may have their heads on one side, they may look very severe (when people are interested their facial muscles relax). Their pupils might be dilated, they may suddenly lean forward or back, they may nod or stroke their faces (a sign of interest), their eyebrows may be raised or lowered. And how can you tell when they are not listening to you but to the thoughts inside their heads?

They might have their arms folded, they might be staring into space or they may be looking at another person in the audience. (More about this in Chapter 11.)

Active listening on the part of the receiver is imperative at this stage. Active listening means listening all the way through without reacting. Asking for clarification, paying attention to the body language and paralanguage of the sender and encouraging the sender to continue.

Decoding

This is where the receiver tries to make sense of the message. Decoding is very much affected by the same things that affect encoding, but from the audience's point of view. These are education, mother tongue, age, gender, experience, vocabulary, knowledge, status, expertise, secrecy or openness, personality, personal preferences and priorities.

Obviously if the sender *encodes* in the same way that the receiver *decodes* then the message will be well understood!

Responding

This is where the receiver sends their message back and the whole cycle starts again.

Here the responders will be considering the following things:

■ Do we know what we (the receivers), want out of this communication? If the audience does not know what to expect from a presentation they can't be sure what they want to hear and will listen less carefully.

■ Could we ask for clarification when we need it? Will there be time for questions, when will we get a chance to speak?

■ Have we encouraged the sender to keep on talking?

■ Does our body language show that we want the communication to continue?

■ Are we giving enough feedback to keep the communication going on?

■ Are we sticking to the subject?

■ Are we following the social rules of communication?

The golden rule of communication is: *the meaning of the message is the responsibility of the sender, not the receiver.*

The major danger spots in the communication cycle are:

■ non-prioritization of the messages (too much is sent and in the wrong order);

■ poor encoding where the sender pays no attention to the language, experience and decoding needs of the receiver;

■ incongruence between the meaning of the message and the manner in which it is sent;

■ poor delivery mechanisms where the message cannot be heard or seen;

■ poor decoding where the receiver does not ask for clarification of any misunderstandings.

Now let's go back to how the audience is processing the information they are hearing. Apart from their own personality preferences, people's brains also have preferred ways of understanding information. These are *visual*, *aural* and *kinesic*.

Table 4.3 Types of processor

Visual processor	Aural processor	Kinesic processor
Here the eyes are the main gateway to understanding. To the visual processor a picture is truly worth a thousand words, words alone are not enough.	Here the ears are the main gateway to understanding. They need to not only hear, but discuss what they have heard If they don't they will not fully understand it.	Here there is a need for D.I.Y. – trying it out for themselves, tasting it, feeling it, doing it. Input is through doing. Kinesics often find it hard to sit still for long.

This is how each processor makes sense of information.

Table 4.4 Processors taking in information

Activity	Visuals	Aurals	Kinesics
Learning	Learns by looking, watching demonstrations, pictures	Learns by listening to others, likes discussion	Learns by doing, likes physical involvement
Written matter	Loves vivid descriptions, concentrates very hard	Loves spoken drama, not particularly interested in illustrations	Likes to be told what to do, probably fidgets when reading, not an avid reader

Table 4.4 continued

Activity	Visuals	Aurals	Kinesics
Remembering	Faces not names, takes notes, likes visual aids like mind mapping	Names not faces, needs verbal repetition	Remembers what was done, not what they saw or heard
Imagining	Thinks in pictures, detailed visualization	Thinks in sounds, subvocalizes 'mm hmmm,'	Pictures not important, often gestures to help remember
Distracted by	Physical disorder and people moving about	Background noise, music	Often looks generally inattentive
Problem solving	Very deliberate, plans in advance, makes lists and writes things down	Talks problems out, often talks to self	Attacks the problem physically. Often picks the solution involving the most activity
Inactivity	Looks around, finds something to watch, doodles	Talks to self or others	Finds a way to move around
New situations	Examines surroundings, looks at handouts	Talks about the situation	Tries things out, touches and fiddles with things
Emotions	Glares when angry, grins when happy, face very expressive	Blows up verbally, expresses emotion verbally, calms down quickly	Gestures, moves hands and limbs to express emotion
Communication	Often quiet, may not talk at length, impatient when has to listen for too long	Likes listening but can't wait to talk. Likes hearing self and others talk	Gestures when speaking, does not seem to listen well, stands close when listening
Vocabulary	'see', 'look', 'watch', 'imagine', 'I'll be seeing you'.	'listen', 'hear', 'sounds like', 'I'll give you a ring'.	'get', 'feel', 'touch', 'I'll be in touch'.

Within any audience you will have a mixture of these thinking styles. If you can bear this in mind when putting your presentation together, you will be seen as a skilled presenter. Make sure there are enough pictures, diagrams, imagery and descriptions for the visuals, enough discussion points, chances to speak, exact language and verbal information for the aurals and enough activity for the kinesics (give them something to fiddle with if you can).

I once went to an incredible presentation that showed how this could be done. The speaker was head of design for a well-known racing team. He was giving a factory tour, explaining just why his team was winning and describing the new technology the team was using. We started off in the entrance hall where he showed us a map of the factory and gave us all a cup of coffee. We were standing next to a real racing car (as driven by the world champion and smelling deliciously of oil). All the team's trophies were on glittering display. He told us when the team was formed and how it was funded. Then he took questions and after that, started the tour. We saw everything and were encouraged to handle the things that interested us (as far as this was safely possible). We looked at the computer screens, plans and diagrams in the design offices, the lathes and machinery in the production departments and the assembly plant.

Throughout the two hours (which passed very quickly) anyone could ask any questions they wanted to, while the quieter members of the audience could examine the equipment and components. All in all the entire audience was completely happy with the presentation and all in all the thinking styles, personalities and interests of the audience were completely satisfied and that is what we should be aiming for when we make a presentation.

Summary

If we take only our own learning preferences and mental processes into consideration when we plan and deliver our presentations, then we are short-changing the people in the audience who don't learn and think like us. You can guarantee that you will have all three listening styles in the audience – the As who like to hear facts and examples and who don't like being hurried, the Bs who are enthusiastic and like to work fast and the Cs who need to discuss. Cater for each of these and the whole audience will be happy. Also think about how people process information, using vivid pictures and images for the visuals, hard facts and excellent words for the aurals and something that the kinesics can hold and touch.

Keep in mind the rules for good communication – always remember that the meaning of the message is entirely the responsibility of the sender.

5

How People Remember, What They Forget

If people are to act on what we have presented to them then what we have said must be remembered – for several days if possible.

There are basically four stages of memory – ultra short-term, short-term, medium-term and long-term, and in order to get information into our long-term memory (which is where we store information that we are familiar with and use often) we must go through the first three stages. The problem with presentations is that they are linear – they progress from start to end, rather like a long passing train, which can mean that by the time we get to the guard's van we have almost certainly forgotten the number of the train.

Paying attention to how the audience's memory works when we construct a presentation will pay great dividends.

The four stages of memory

The ultra short-term memory gateway (in presentation terms this is the start of each major point in the presentation) is the gateway to remembering. It doesn't hold much and it lasts for a very short time indeed. Nonetheless, information must pass through this gateway in order to be processed. We use our senses to open this gateway – we see, touch, smell, taste or hear whatever the information is.

From the list below, what are the things that you remember best?

spoken words	black and white	written words
pictures	photographs	sounds
smells	feelings	rhyme
music	actions	texture
tastes	colours	places

We all have our own preferences but sad to say, the first three – spoken words, written words and black and white are the least effective ways of making people remember – and yet these are usually the three things presenters use – the speech, the handouts and those boring visuals!

Depending on how the information is presented, and to a certain extent our own memory preferences, some ways of presenting are easier to remember than others. Seeing something is often more memorable than just hearing about it, tasting or smelling something very often leaves a stronger impression than just hearing about it, and, particularly in the case of manual skills, touching and doing something will be more effective than just listening. It is also true that the more senses that are involved in processing new information the stronger will be the memories associated with that information.

The formation of memory is a complex chemical process, which needs to be kick-started by presenting new information three times at the very least, so it is important to gain the audience's attention and interest right from the start.

There is one other very significant fact about the ultra short-term memory – it is all too easy to jam up the gateway with too much information. Seven facts or fewer is all it can cope with at once – any more and the brain becomes confused and all information is lost. This is why it is absolutely counterproductive to present too many facts at once; the audience simply will not be able to process them and will become mentally tired and rather irritable.

So what does all this information about the ultra short-term memory gateway mean? It means that we should carefully structure the way we present information to an audience right from the very start. Here's an example: you have been asked to present the plans for a complex office relocation to the 12 people in your department. They only know that they will be moving, and nothing yet about where they are going or when. You are also aware that they have concerns about the move.

You could start with (1) an overview slide or handout of a colourful map that shows the location of the new office in relation to the current office. Follow this with (2) a slide showing the address of the new office and the date when the move is to take place. Then (3) show a detailed plan of the new office itself (with the address clearly stated in words on the slide). This will push the information through the audience's ultra short-term memory gateway and on to the next stage.

The short-term memory is next. This is more capacious, and lasts a little longer. It is somewhat like a sieve; any information that the audience isn't interested in or believes to be untruthful will be sieved out, whereas anything that the audience finds useful and truthful will be retained. Here the audience decides whether the new input is of any use. The short-term memory is easily bored, has a small capacity, is short-lived and very judgemental. It is useful to remember that if you are presenting information that the audience may feel uncomfortable with or alarmed by, they will stop listening to you and start listening to their own internal thoughts.

In presentation terms this is where you develop each point with examples, comparisons, illustrations and references to what is already known. In terms of our example of the office move, here you could show plans of the offices as they exist now, showing what will be actually moved, and plans of the future office showing where the office furniture and fittings will be placed. This handles the information needs of the presentation, but there are other needs you should consider. How does the audience feel about the move? What concerns will they have? Any significant change causes concern to an audience, even if they know the change will be advantageous in the end.

Because the short-term memory acts as a sieve, the audience will be worrying about how the move will affect them personally (will I get a desk by a window? What about parking? Will there be a canteen? How far is the new office from the shops? How will I cope with both my workload and the move?). They will be choosing what to remember and what to ignore. At this point it is useful to relate the information directly to each individual it will affect. Using people's names focuses their attention and drives the message home.

Having put across this information as personally as you can, you have now engaged the short-term memory.

The best way to move the new information completely through the short-term memory sieve is to get people talking about what they have learned, so, if you then ask the audience if anyone knows anything about the area where the new office is located, or if they have any concerns, they will start internalizing the new information and deciding how important it is to them. To treat the short-term memory kindly you need to think about them personally, hook new information to old, stress what is important and give examples. If you do this successfully then you will have navigated the audience through the short-term memory sieve and into the medium-term working memory.

The medium-term working memory is next. It is extremely active and lively. Here new memories are compared with old. It is where the brain really begins to work with the new information. It swings between existing memories and the new information. This is what we aim for in presentations. The medium-term working memory is quite capacious and the memories it holds can last for up to a week although they will need reinforcement. Again, discussion helps to reinforce the medium-term memory, as do plenty of examples and pictures. In presentation terms, this is where you present alternatives, give the audience choices, get them to think about what they will do with this new information.

Back to our example of the office move; the new information is in, personal concerns have been addressed, and now you can move that information through the medium-term memory by looking at the logistics and possible pitfalls of the move. You could draw up a slide showing (graphically if possible) the detailed timetable of the move, you could collect a list of risks and dangers from the audience, using a flip chart (this makes a refreshing change from looking at a screen and involves the audience directly). You could even break the audience into sub groups and ask them to come up with a solution to the dangers on the risk list. By the time you have done all this you should have a committed audience who can remember the main points of what you have said and who will willingly move that information into their long-term memories.

The long-term reinforced memory is the final stage. This is a vast and mysterious place – all our embedded skills and knowledge are stored there. Rather like dried flowers, the colours may fade but the structure of the memory stays the same. It would be wonderful if we could get information into the audience's long-term memory during a presentation – however this is unlikely to happen since it takes several days of thinking, manipulating and using information before it is permanently stored. What we can do though, is to make a 'call to action' at the end of the presentation that will encourage the audience to think and talk about what they have heard in the days or weeks following the actual presentation.

Back to our example, your final slides need to sum up what you want them to remember about the move. Don't overload them with information, just put up the essentials in as colourful and memorable a way as possible. The final reminder should be your call to action, that is, a statement of exactly what you want them to do next. Maybe a flip chart of who does what, or a listing of what needs to be considered. To further reinforce what you have said it would be useful to provide them with a comprehensive handout containing all the information you have covered that they can read at their leisure.

To summarize so far: when you put a presentation together it is vital to pay attention to the way the memory works – there is no point in trying to cram too many facts into an unsuspecting audience. To start the memory process you must lead them through the ultra short-term memory gateway by presenting each piece of information three times (show, tell, explain)

Associations and differences

Associations are things like: smell, taste, sounds, surroundings, state of mind, location, and physical state. The more associations we make when we are learning something, the easier it is to remember. We rummage

Figure 5.1   What we remember well and what we remember badly

around our memories to find these associations when we need to remember things, so making the presentation room as comfortable, interesting and memorable as you can, will bring a set of associations to the presentation that will fix it in their minds.

Let's look at that list again:

spoken words	black and white	written words
pictures	photographs	sounds
smells	feelings	rhyme
music	actions	texture
tastes	colours	places

Read through the list at the top of the page, then shut your eyes and try to remember everything that was on it (impossible, I know, bearing in mind how much the ultra short-term and short-term memory can hold). However it is likely that you did remember 'pictures', 'actions', 'rhyme' and 'tastes'. Why? Because they were different, they stood out from the rest of the list. Making a difference in the way you present information will help your audience to remember what you have said. So what differences do you have at your disposal?

- ▓ You could make it *brighter*. You could use a bright picture on a slide, brighter lettering, a brighter tone of voice.
- ▓ You could make it *louder* or *softer*. Using stress and volume will make the audience sit up, using pause and softness will make them listen harder and therefore remember better.
- ▓ You could change position. This is particularly effective if you are penned up behind a lectern. The audience gets bored looking at exactly the same background, so changing your position on the stage livens them up.

■ You could involve the audience. Asking a direct question of the audience or asking them to contribute will refresh them and make them think about what you have said.

■ You could use a different media. As with changing position, the audience can easily become torpid looking at the screen all the time. You could use a flip chart, or even change from a static screen to a video clip or voice recording.

■ You could take a short break. This is very effective. The audience has the chance to internalize what you have said – even better if you can get them to discuss what you have said with their neighbours. When the audience participates they have a chance to relate what you have said to their own experience.

■ You could change speakers. Bringing in an expert or someone with a terrific story to tell backs up your message effectively.

Now, a word about company templates and typefaces. With all the previous advice about making a difference in order to be memorable, how does this fit with the company's desire to have recognizable and badged presentations, where the constant background and typography mitigates against difference? Well, it means that you really do have to think about how to make each slide count, otherwise they are going to slip by in an unending stream of similarity. Imagine the tedium of two or three slideshows back to back, each with identical typography and layout! There's more about this in the next chapter.

Numerical information

For most of us, numbers in themselves are not memorable. Look at this statement (the speaker is talking about the opportunities for his company in the existing export market):

> Last year we shipped two thousand tonnes to Belgium, two thousand tonnes to Iceland, two thousand tonnes to Luxemburg, two thousand tonnes to Finland and twenty thousand tonnes to Sweden.

What is the point the speaker is making? That Belgium, Iceland, Luxembourg and Finland are the opportunity since they are not buying as much as Sweden? Or that Sweden is the opportunity because it is buying ten times as much as the others? Does the actual tonnage matter?

The bald statement of numerical facts is not usually enough to make the message memorable; it is how these facts are interpreted:

> An exciting opportunity exists for us in Belgium, Iceland, Luxembourg and Finland. They are buying only one-tenth of the tonnage that Sweden buys, and yet all of these countries have the same need for raw materials.

If you have a vivid backup slide showing these figures as a chart then the audience will remember them well.

Breaking numeric information into digestible chunks makes it memorable because the mind remembers the number of chunks rather than being put off by the total amount of information. The way we remember telephone numbers is an example of this. Take any 11-digit number, e.g. 01775 493943, and break it down into its component parts:

The beginning chunk, 01, tells you it is a British telephone number, 775 tells you which part of the country it is in, 49 tells you which town it is in and the last four digits (3942) is the actual number. This gives you (01) (775) (49) (3943), four chunks, which is easier to remember than 11 separate digits.

Equally, if people can find a pattern in the things they need to remember, this makes it easier to retain the memories. This is why mnemonics work so well. For example: 'Richard Of York Gave Battle In Vain' gives you red, orange, yellow, green, blue, indigo and violet (the colours of the spectrum), and 'How I wish I could ascertain' by looking at the number of letters in each word gives you 3, 1, 4, 1, 5, 9, the value of Pi (π).

Exercise

You are giving a presentation on the financial standing of your company. The year-end figures are splendid. Profits are up, costs are down, the market is booming, the pension fund is hugely in profit and the value of the company's real estate portfolio is growing by the day. The shareholders in the audience are going to be really pleased. How can you prevent the recital of all these numbers from becoming boring?

There are other factors that will make a presentation really unmemorable, in fact the things listed here will cause people to actively forget: an inaudible voice talking about unrelated facts in a negative way using commonplace words and clichés are guaranteed to make the audience want to forget your presentation. Try to make the words you use vivid, personally involving, colourful, quirky and descriptive. Modulate your voice and use gestures to make your meaning clear.

Exercise

Find alternatives for the following:

Big	Useful	Powerful	State-of-the-art
User-friendly	Latest	Capacity	Value
Fast	Platform	Comprehensive	Leverage

Primacy and recency effect

Finally, there are several physical things that you can to do reinforce memory. In any learning session the first and last parts are remembered best. This is called the 'primacy and recency effect'. To take advantage of this, state your main message up front as well as at the finish.

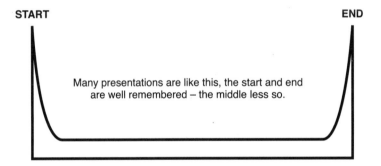

Figure 5.2   Primacy and recency effect

Taking breaks also increases the primacy and recency effect.

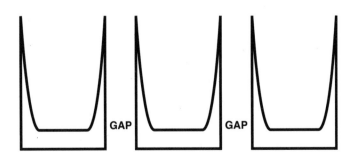

Figure 5.3   Taking breaks

Three breaks triple the effect.

There is a burst of memory energy a short time after learning, and frequent breaks and changes of pace capitalize on this. Don't spend longer than 20 minutes on a subject (even a one-minute break for a stretch can help). Every 40 minutes, take a complete break of no less than 10 minutes. When you restart, recap quickly about where you were and add an example of what you were talking about. The re-enlivened audience will have a sudden memory burst and be even more receptive to the rest of the presentation.

Summary

Bearing all these factors in mind, you will see that it is not enough to know your audience's interests – you also need to consider their personalities and the way their brains work. The process of human memory is a complicated business and this too must be taken into account when putting your presentation together.

6

Selecting Your Subject and Organizing Your Information

The pre-scripting phase of preparing a presentation is where you have the chance to experiment. Obviously you need to know what you are trying to achieve, and what the audience wants, but you still have the problem of how to make your presentation stand out.

Imagine this: you are the spokesman for a large chain of supermarkets. You have been asked to give a presentation to a group of journalists. What are you going to talk about?

That's a pretty wide remit, and you've only got 30 minutes for the presentation. You can't possibly talk about everything you know – for one thing this would probably take months, and for another the audience simply wouldn't stand for it. So you have to choose your subject.

Now add another factor into the mix. There have been terrible floods in the Midlands and crops are severely affected. The pea crop is destroyed, potato fields are under water and have been so for two weeks, it is harvest time and the dreadful ground conditions mean that the wheat and corn cannot be gathered in. Shortages of water, vegetables and bread are already happening in the towns most severely affected by the floods because the delivery lorries can't get through to them.

Now you have more of an idea about what to say. The audience will not want to hear about the splendid new tills you have installed at all your branches. They will not be in any way interested in the fact that you have developed a new training scheme for school leavers, or indeed care if you have made enormous profits over the last financial year. What do they want to hear about?

Another scenario: you are the leader of a small project team. The project will start up tomorrow. The new team members (who have been involved in projects before) do not know each other or very much about the project itself. You have called a meeting of the entire team and the project sponsors. This meeting can take as long as you like over the space of a morning (9.00–12.30). What will you cover at this meeting?

Setting SMART objectives

The bedrock of a good presentation is the material that you will cover. Too much and people become confused. Too little and they feel short-changed. As the last two chapters showed, audience research is the key, but you will still have to rummage through your own knowledge base to pick the subjects and the aspects of those subjects that will keep the audience happy. To do this you need to set your objectives for the presentation clearly. Successful objectives must be SMART:

▓ simple enough to be expressed in one or two short sentences;
▓ measurable by the success criteria you have set;
▓ achievable within the boundaries of what you can do;
▓ realistic in terms of your time scales and resources;
▓ timed.

First, think about what you are actually trying to do with your presentation. It may be one or many of the following:

Selling	Instructing	Introducing	Image making
Providing a choice	Persuading	Scene setting	Damage control
Updating	Information cascading	Giving good news	Giving bad news
Amusing	Motivating	Correcting	

Then look back to your audience research and find out why they are attending the presentation.

Work out how you are going to measure whether you have achieved your first objective or not. Will the question and answer session show that the audience has got the message? Will you test the audience? Will you have a questionnaire at the end, with a debrief of selected members of the audience?

Next, look back over similar presentations that you or your colleagues have given and see if what you are trying to do is achievable, bearing in mind the time you have to deliver the presentation and the mind set that the audience will bring to the presentation.

Then have a look at the amount of time you can set aside for preparing and organizing the presentation, finding, persuading and briefing other speakers, gathering the information you will need and rehearsing.

Finally, set a realistic timescale for the presentation itself. Will 20 minutes speaking and 10 minutes for questions be enough? Will you need more time, and if so how can you break the presentation up into 20-minute sections with good links between the sections?

Exercise

What objectives might you set for the supermarket spokesman's presentation?

When you have set and checked your objectives you can then work out what must be included, what would be useful to back these facts up, what is unnecessary and what you should definitely not talk about at all.

Exercise

The project manager needs to set her objectives for the first meeting with her team. What might they be?

Having set the objectives, here are some of the things that the project manager (a real expert on project management) was thinking about putting into her 40-minute presentation to her new team:

■ the history of project management;

■ projects that she had run in the past (all successful!);

■ details of the new project: project objectives, project parameters;

■ details about the client;

■ the project methodology to be used;

■ the importance of the project to the company;

■ an 'introduce yourself' session so people get to know each other (after the main presentation);

■ allocation of roles within the project;

■ how the project will benefit the project team;

- difficulties the team might encounter with the project;
- past projects that the company has messed up;
- introduction of the project sponsors;
- what will happen to the team if they fail with this project.

Note, that at this point you are just working out general points and not going into any detail.

Should she talk about all of them? Some of them will fulfil the objectives and some might hinder it. Some information is unnecessary at this stage and some is vital. Some information will make the time scales impossible. Edit the list and then prioritize it.

Exercise

You have been asked to give a presentation to a group of keen gardeners about suitable plants for today's gardens. You have 30 minutes, 10 of which will be used for questions. The hot topic of the moment is the impact of global warming and how drier summers have led to the need for drought-resistant plants. What might you include in your presentation, bearing in mind that you have only 20 minutes?

You not only have to select what you are going to say, you also need to think about how you will organize what you are going to say. There are several ways of doing this. The garden expert might choose to arrange his information into grouped items – flowers that grow in bright sunlight, flowers that grow in dry shade and flowers that grow in both. He could then divide these items into subgroups. Thus:

Table 6.1 Planting times

		Main Groups			
Dry, bright sunlight		Dry, cooler shade		Shade and sunlight	
Flowering plants	Foliage plants	Flowering plants	Foliage plants	Flowering plants	Foliage plants
When to plant | When to plant	When to plant | When to plant	When to plant | When to plant	When to plant | When to plant	When to plant | When to plant	When to plant | When to plant

The spokesman for the supermarket might well choose a 'time-scale' organization where he talks about what has happened, what is happening at the moment and what will happen in the future. Thus:

Table 6.2 Past, present and future

What has happened in the past	What's happening now	What will happen in the future
Local area flooded, regional supplies limited, rationing for some items	Importing supplies from further away, some temporary price rises, no rationing	Return to local suppliers, no rationing, everything back to normal

The project manager might choose a problem-solving approach where she looks at what needs to be done, how it is going to be done and who is involved.

Table 6.3 Problem-solving approach

What needs to be done	How this will be done	Who will be involved
1. Fully understand project parameters and client needs	1. Interrogate project statements, hold meeting with client, starting tomorrow	1. Everyone
2. Fully understand the importance of the project to the company	2. Presentation from project sponsor, Thursday	2. Project sponsor, everyone
3. Etc.	3. Etc.	3. Etc.

Organization methods

Whichever way you organize your information you will need to tell the audience how you are going to present the information to them. This gives them a structure to help them understand and will set their expectations clearly. At this point you are not writing the script, merely deciding what is going into it. You may well find after you have started to think about your subject (and I often do) that the organization method that you have chosen doesn't exactly fit. In that case, try another method until you are satisfied – after all you haven't started on the script yet and so haven't wasted much time at all.

Other options for organizing your information are as follows:

■ The 'question, answer and significance' approach (an example that could be used by the supermarket spokesman).

Table 6.4 Question, answer and significance approach

Question	Answer	Significance
What has happened to the supply of bottled water to the supermarkets within a radius of 20 miles?	There has been an enormous demand and supplies are running low for the next day or so. Supplies will be back to normal by Thursday	Bottled water will be rationed to 3 litres per purchaser until Thursday
If the pea crop has failed, what will this do to the availability of frozen peas?	The big suppliers of frozen peas will be importing peas from European markets	There will probably be a price rise when current stocks are sold

■ 'Contrast and compare'. This is very useful when giving a selling and demonstrating presentation. Here is an example for a company's new graphic design package:

Table 6.5 Contrast and compare

Fact/feature of our package	The way things were	The way we do things now	How we beat our competitors	Benefit of using our package
100 type fonts	Only 12 type fonts on the old WP package	All new fonts are fully compatible with every other WP package on the market	No one else uses so many true type fonts	No problems with any printers on the market, complete freedom of choice
Text and graphics can be highly condensed	Limited ability to condense large documents	This is done automatically	The only other package that can condense is 50% less effective	Saves time when composing documents, saves time and money when sending by broadband

■ 'Let me tell you a story'. This works well for 'motherhood and apple pie' presentations when you are presenting the history and credibility of your company. It is loosely based on the format of a traditional tale. Starting at 'once upon a time' and ending with 'they all lived happily ever-after' although probably not in those exact words. It gives you a structure to hang your information on. Think about the ingredients of a good yarn. The arrival of the hero, the arrival of the villain, the quest for the grail, the wicked stepmother, the slaying of the dragon, the magic spell, and use these in the narrative. You could equally choose the plot of a play or a film and base your presentation on this.

To summarize: it is at this point, before starting to script the presentation that you need the chance to play around with ideas. Start by defining just what you are going to cover and how you are going to do this. Too much information and they will not be able to remember it all, too little and the audience will feel unsatisfied. Setting clear objectives will help with this. Objectives must be SMART if you are going to achieve them. Having set your objectives you can now list, prioritize and organize the information you are going to present into 'must know', 'helps to understand', 'nice to know', 'not necessary' and 'positively damaging'. Now think about how you are going to organize that information in a way that will make it completely understandable and interesting to the audience. Until you have thought all this through you are not ready to begin scripting.

A final exercise

You are the head of HR in a well-liked local company who is running a recruitment drive for school leavers. You have decided to use the 'let me tell you a story' approach to present your company's history. Choose one of the following to base your story on:

■ a fairy story, (e.g. Cinderella and the ugly sisters, The Three Billy Goats Gruff, Rumpelstiltskin, etc);

■ a film, (e.g. *Star Wars*, *Top Gun*, *Shrek*, *Harry Potter*, etc);

■ a play or a musical (e.g. anything from Shakespeare, any pantomime, *Peter Pan*, etc).

Lark about with this and see what you can achieve.

7

Writing the Script

Having researched your audience and selected your subjects you are now ready to write your script. Before you do anything else you will have decided just exactly what it is you want to achieve using the SMART objectives formula.

So let's take another example. You have been asked to make a presentation to a group of new employees on the use of fire extinguishers in each department. You know that one-third of the audience will be joining the pre-sales team, one-third of the audience will be joining the help desk team and the last third will be working in the stores department. You have been given a morning for the chalk-and-talk and demonstrations. You work for human resources and have the services of the local fire department at your beck and call. The presentation will take place in the lecture hall and outside the hall where there is a fire tank and demonstration equipment.

The objectives are:

- to make sure that all new employees are familiar with and know how to use the right extinguisher in case of any fire;
- to encourage all new employees to be aware of the health and safety regulations relating to fires, particularly in their departments;
- to fulfil the legal requirement to present this information.

Are the objectives simple? Yes.

Are they measurable? Yes – you can get all of them to actually use the fire extinguishers and observe for yourself that they are handling them correctly.

Are they achievable? Yes, this has been done before.

Are they realistic in terms of resources and time scales? Yes, you will only be talking about four different types of extinguisher and you have the fire service to back you up.

Timescale? Yes.

Now you need to collect together all the information you are going to use. You will have done this in general in the selection of subjects, but here you need to go into much more detail. Here you need to ask yourself several questions:

■ What information must I cover – exactly?

■ What am I not going to cover – and why not?

■ Which are the most important points – exactly – itemize them?

■ Which facts will add most value – itemize these?

■ What examples can I use – make these as real as possible?

In the case of information, write each subject that you are going to cover on an index card with the related facts and examples underneath them. You can then try different arrangements of the facts until you feel you have prioritized them.

Now you need a structure to work with. Having a structure will speed up the preparation of the script, keep you on track and help the audience to listen and remember what you have said.

Structuring a script

Like a good novel, play or film, a script needs a beginning, middle and end. To catch your audience's interest and attention you need to start with a bang, to keep their attention and help them to understand you need to give relevant and interesting examples and case studies, and to help them to remember you need to make a good summary at the end.

Because we all work under pressure, I find it very useful to start at the end – by doing this you have the advantage of knowing exactly where you are going and what you are going to cover. The elements of a good ending are:

■ A 'call to action' where you ask the audience to do something that will make them think about what you have told them.

■ A summary of the main points that you have covered – not just a list of the points, but a vivid and memorable reminder of the most important facts.

■ A question-and-answer session. You will need to consider what questions might be asked and what concerns your presentation has raised.

■ A final summary and graceful finish.

Exercise

You are part of the human resources department of a large merchant bank. You are talking to the IT department about the closure of the Huddersfield IT centre, which will be relocated to London. The audience is in no danger of losing their jobs but changes will have to be made. Specifically there will be an increased workload over the near future and an expansion of the department into the suite of offices next to the existing computer rooms. Within six months everything will settle down and things will become less hectic. This is brand new news to the audience. These are the general points you need to have covered in the presentation:

■ the advantages of the relocation of the IT centre to London;
■ job security and increase in salaries;
■ changes in working patterns and workload;
■ office expansion and timetable;
■ opportunities for all.

Plan the ending to your presentation, including a call to action.

In the case of the health and safety presentation the final summary might cover the labelling of flammable items, the different types of fire that might be encountered and the actual use of the extinguishers. The question-and-answer session will undoubtedly raise concerns about personal danger and the likelihood of particular types of fire in particular locations. The 'call to action' might be a request for everyone in the audience to search out the warning signs, fire risks and fire escapes in their departments.

Write the detailed points for the ending on index cards and prioritize them.

With the end sorted out, you now go back to the beginning. Here you need to catch their attention immediately. There are many ways of doing this – a startling statistic, a current news story, a pertinent quote, an amazing picture, a fact completely related to your audience or their company that allows you to use their name or company name.

Introduce yourself and set the audience's expectations about your expertise positively. This is sometimes known as the 'credibility statement'. It tells them why you are qualified to speak on the subject and what your background is. It also allows you to put your contact details up on the screen if you are using one; if so, the contact details slide will also be needed at the end of the presentation.

Introduce your topics and show why they are important.
State your conclusions.
Write each of these elements in detail onto separate index cards and prioritize them.

Exercise

Prepare a short introduction of yourself (approximately 500 words). You need to cover what you do, your past experience, what your interests are and what you hope to do in the future. Try to make it light hearted and try to relate it to the audience.

Now to the middle of the presentation. Here you are giving evidence to support the information you are putting across. This could take many forms – case studies that show in real terms how what you are talking about could be applied, demonstrations that prove the truth of what you are telling them and examples of how what you are telling them will be useful. Write your ideas down on separate index cards and prioritize them.

Logic and flow: each of the points you make should lead on to the next one – if you jump about from subject to subject with no apparent link the audience will become confused. This logical flow must go through everything you are going to say. You can do this by using a little test. Look over your ideas on the index cards and test the flow between them by saying 'This means that ...', 'and then ...', or 'therefore ...', and work out how they do actually link together.

Get the bones of the presentation sorted out before you start writing the actual words.

Exercise

You have been asked to give a presentation to the IT department of a company who have just bought a new software suite from your company. These are the facts you need to cover:

■ It will take three days to reconfigure the old system.
■ There must be at least 20Mb of disk-space free.
■ It needs 60Mb of memory.

■ ABCTurbo will be installed on the Server and access by other users will be controlled by passwords.
■ All dumb terminals must be logged off during the installation.
■ The System Controller will need 3 days' training.
■ The installation will cost £400.
■ ABCTurbo will not run on your system as it is configured at the moment.
■ Extra memory can be purchased at £600 per Mb.
■ You will need a removable hard disk.
■ There is a three-month wait for this software.
■ The training cost is £100.

Put these points into a logical order.

Now you can start to write the actual script.

Scriptwriting rules

Have an interesting title.

Now that you know exactly where the script is going, it is worth trying to find a theme. Themes are an excellent way of keeping the audience on track – as well as linking the presentation's stages. A quick scan of the World Wide Web found a possible theme for the health and safety presentation: 'push, aim, squeeze, sweep', (PASS), which is the acronym the fire service uses to help people to remember the sequence of actions needed when using a fire extinguisher. This could become the title as well as the theme of the presentation.

The title should not only reflect what the presentation is about but also give some idea of the approach the presentation is going to take.

Exercise

Here are the titles of three actual presentations that I have attended. See if you can come up with something more effective for each of them.

■ 'Plans for 2004': This was a presentation from the CEO of a small company that was in the process of an aggressive takeover by their biggest rival. No redundancies were expected, but huge changes were about to happen.

■ 'Legal Requirements Relating to Clause 24': This was a presentation from a company lawyer regarding changes to the way contracts were drawn up.

■ 'Customer Satisfaction': This was a presentation from the sales director of a company who had just received the results of a damaging customer survey.

Having found a snappy title, think about the script itself. There are five major rules that you should keep in mind at all times:

■ Do not introduce evidence that you cannot substantiate. The more you use examples and case studies the better.

■ Steer as clear from jargon as you can. Even though you are utterly familiar with it, you cannot be sure that your audience will be. This is particularly true of acronyms, which seem to be spattered throughout all technical presentations. If you are going to use an acronym, abbreviation or technical term, explain what it means in full the first time you use it.

■ Think about how your audience will respond to every point you make. If you are going to say something contentious or something that may upset the audience, you will need to consider what they will be thinking about. Heavy thinking tends to make people deaf, so use pauses and careful punctuation to allow people sufficient time to mull over what you have said.

■ Be ruthless with your editing. Less is always more: it's no good overloading the audience with too many facts (see Chapter 5).

■ When you move from one subject to the other, put in an introductory sentence to show that you are moving on to another topic.

Before looking at style and vocabulary, a word about timing. Most people speak at about 140–150 words per minute. That means that an A40 sheet of paper, printed at 12 points, ranged left and double spaced and containing approximately 370 words, will take just over two-and-a-half minutes to speak. So a 20-minute speech means approximately eight pages of script or nearly 3,000 words. (Not that I would ever recommend reading a script word for word).

Style and vocabulary

George Orwell, who knew a thing or two about writing, said the following:

■ Never use a metaphor, simile or other figure of speech that you are used to seeing in print.

■ Never use a long word when a short one will do.

■ If it is possible to cut a word out, always do so.

■ Never use the passive where you can use the active.

■ Never use a foreign phrase, a scientific word or a jargon word if you can think of an everyday English equivalent.

■ Break any of the rules sooner than say anything that is downright barbarous.

In other words, keep an eye out for the sort of business-speak that comes and goes in and out of fashion. Examples include things like 'leveraging the sale', 'coming down the turnpike', 'proactive management', and so on. These are probably not words or phrases that you would use in normal conversation but they do seem to creep pompously into presentations.

The only real test is to speak your words out loud while you are writing them. If you find it hard to say them, or they don't sound like the sort of thing you would normally say then turn them into something that you can easily say and that sounds like you. The written word and the spoken word are not always the same, and perfectly good speakers sometimes turn into pedantic and condescending presenters who have no credibility whatsoever when they're over-scripted.

Exercise

Very often we use several words where one or two would do. This is bad practice in presentations since it unnecessarily clouds up the communication. Here are some examples, next to each of them write the shorter version.

Longer version	Short version
In a very few cases	_____
Has a tendency to	_____
It is obvious that	_____
In the vicinity of	_____

For the reason of   _____

In the event of   _____

Have a dialogue   _____

Take into consideration   _____

It will be noticed that   _____

Pompous words   **Simpler version**

Assist   _____

Locate   _____

Procure   _____

Commence   _____

Terminate   _____

Elevate   _____

Aggravate   _____

Behove   _____

Jargon   **Clarity**

Empowerment   _____

Platform   _____
(Add your own here.)

The script is nearly complete. Now you need to go through it ruthlessly and edit it. Anything that does not add value should be cut out. Anything that cannot be substantiated should be cut out. Anything that sounds in the least bit waffly should be cut out. Anything that is boring should be cut out or changed to make it interesting.

Check through the script to see if you really have talked about benefits and not just facts and features. Here are some examples of the difference between facts, features and benefits:

Table 7.1 Facts, features and benefits

Fact (A piece of information)	Feature (Why this is special)	Benefit (What it will actually do for you, personally)
This washing machine spins at 1000 revolutions per minute	This is the fastest spin of any machine on the market	1000 revs means that your clothes are dry in half the time
This car has a super-efficient heater	It heats up the interior in just three minutes	It keeps your feet warm in winter. (Not a benefit if you live on the equator)
This software package allows you to integrate graphics and text	It can be used with any operating system	This allows to you use the package on your existing machines, so saving money

When you are satisfied that you have put everything you need into the script, read it aloud. This is the acid test – if it doesn't feel comfortable, adjust it to make it sound natural.

Reading aloud, sadly doesn't often sound natural. Here's a little test. Turn on the radio and scan through the stations. You will soon spot who is reading their own words aloud and who is speaking without reading from a script. The latter always sound more convincing. Now this doesn't mean that they haven't prepared carefully and are using notes, but it does mean that they know their subject in depth and are getting their points across effectively. They probably have prepared a script to help them get their ideas straight but when it comes to performance time they won't stick rigidly to every single word. This should be the same for you. The script is the skeleton of your presentation, but only that. Working from notes or reminder cards is the best way of getting value from your script. This is how I prepare mine:

Table 7.2   Skeleton on index card (template)

Card Number	Subject	Slide	Punch a hole here and hold cards together with a treasury tag
	1st point		
	2nd point		
	3rd point		
	4th point		
	Anything else you need to remember		

Table 7.3   Skeleton on index card

1	Introduction	Title Slide (1)	●
	Welcome to the presentation		
	Show them today's headline		
	Logistics, Credibility statement		
	What they will get out of the presentation		
	(slow down, speak up and keep the eye contact up)		

The script is in your head and the note cards will keep you on track.

The final thing to prepare is the handout. This is where you reinforce your message and should include detailed information that expands on what you have said in the presentation. Make the title page as interesting as possible. If the information is confidential say so at the top of each page. Put contact information (name, title, company name, address, telephone and e-mail) on the title page.

A word about agendas: I am in two minds about them. On the one hand it is a very good thing to set the audience's expectations about what you will cover, but on the other it may well be a signal to the audience about what will bore them and how long they may have to wait for what they really want to hear. For this reason I never present agendas as a sequential list. You could try using a mind map to show how all the items you are going to cover are linked. This mind map shows the agenda for a presentation on Bid Management.

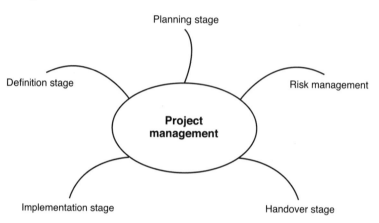

Figure 7.1 Mind map for Bid Management presentation

In summary, scripts need a beginning, a middle and an end.

Table 7.4 Structuring your script

BEGINNING	MIDDLE	END
• Start with a bang, catch their attention, get them to listen actively • Introduce yourself and make a credibility statement • Tell them what you are going to tell them • Show you understand their concerns, tell them why it is worth listening • State your conclusions	• Introduce each point in logical order • Use examples, reference sites, case studies, war stories to illustrate each point • Back up difficult information with a visual • Link each point • Make your language vivid • Keep the pace up	• Summarize the important points and point out why they are important • Make a call to action to reinforce their memories • Run the question and answer session • Recap your call to action • Sign off gracefully • End with a bang and not a whimper

Structuring your script makes it easy for you to remember and easy for the audience to follow what you are saying.

8

Visuals

Bearing in mind all the factors affecting the way people remember and forget, there is a good argument for some kind of a visual reinforcement to what you are saying. This section looks at how we see, ways of using visuals, how to put a layered set of visuals together and general rules that will make slides easy to look at and understand.

Our eyes are amazing, but even they have limits. You need to bear these limits in mind when preparing visuals.

Brightness and afterimage

Beware of bright, white screens, particularly modern screens, which are luminescent and far, far brighter than anything else in the presentation room. Look at the pattern below for a minute or so and then close your eyes and see what happens:

Figure 8.1 Crosshatch pattern

Did you see the crosshatch pattern from the diagram on your eyelids? This is the afterimage caused by a sort of retinal 'burn out' which happens when looking at highly contrasting images. And yet how often do you see presentation slides with black letters on a white background? Possibly people think that because we are used to reading black type on white pages, this is what people would like in a presentation. In fact using a white background will cause eyestrain in the audience. Not severe eyestrain, but enough to tire the audience's eyes. Try different coloured backgrounds with white lettering and see which is easier on the eye.

Speaking of backgrounds, take a look at this:

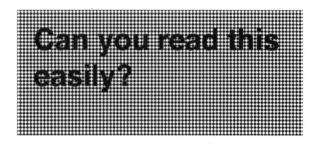

Figure 8.2   Reading test 1

Here, the eyes don't know which to concentrate on – the background or the lettering –and so switch between one and the other. Again, this is a strain on the eyes. Even though some of the packages available for slide production contain a variety of backgrounds (indeed one of the most popular ones has no less than 54 patterned and textured backgrounds that can be selected, in a dizzying range of colours) it doesn't mean you have to use them.

And what about this?

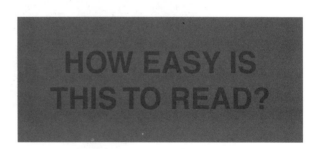

Figure 8.3   Reading test 2

Too little contrast between the lettering and the background is as bad as too much. And what about the colourblind in the audience? This is more common than most people think. Red or blue text on a green or yellow background and vice versa, and similarly the combination of red and blue, are very difficult for colour-blind people to see.

And what about this?

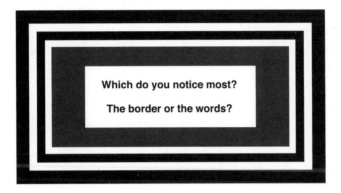

Figure 8.4   Reading test 3

Our peripheral vision is very powerful so steer clear of fancy borders or your message will be overwhelmed.

Westerners read from left to right and so their eyes are used to scanning images in the same way. When using complicated diagrams keep this in mind, and rather than putting the whole complex image up at once, build it up element by element.

When adding text to diagrams, don't be tempted to use vertical text. If there is no room for horizontal text then simplify the diagram.

Figure 8.5   Reading test 4

A word about complicated diagrams and slides. If you really have to put up a slide with a complex diagram on it then you need to introduce it carefully. Before the slide comes up tell the audience what to expect and where to look first. For example, the diagram below contains a great deal of information, so when it comes up on the screen the audience doesn't really know where to look. You could introduce it like this: 'The next slide shows who does what in our organization. You will see that there are three main departments, the largest being finance.' Then bring up the slide and wait three or four seconds for the audience to take it in. If you start talking as soon as the slide comes up the audience will be concentrating on the slide and not listening to you.

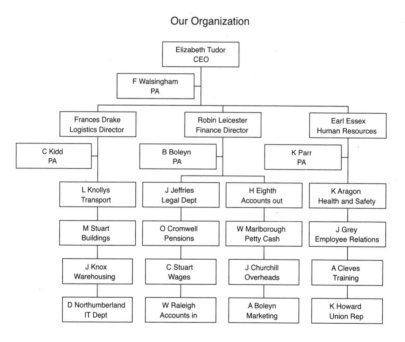

Figure 8.6 Organization structure

Better still, if at all possible, build up a slide by introducing the components one at a time, and then you can make your point even more effectively.

Sight is one of the senses that produces very powerful memories and for many people a picture or a visual representation is essential for them to understand what is being said. Certainly there are several things in a presentation that must be shown in pictures or diagrams:

■ numbers, calculations and budgetary information;
■ spatial information, directions, layouts;

■ direct quotes that must be accurate, like specifications or legal instructions;

■ telephone numbers, contact information and e-mail addresses;

■ names;

■ specifications;

Layout, templates and typefaces

Since the introduction of presentation software, audiences have become very used to looking at slide shows – in fact there is one school of thought that hates them, believing that they make presenters lazy and boring. There is some truth in this. I was at a presentation session given by a supplier of video systems the other month and after three presentations, every single one of which used the same company logo, livery, layout and typeface they all began to blur together.

It is understandable that companies who have spent large amounts on corporate identities will want to get their money's worth, but what does it do to the audience's attention span? One way round this is to have a choice of templates and background colours and to use pictures, images and diagrams as much as possible since there is nothing deadlier than having a presenter reading what is on the screen as if the audience were full of pre-reading infants.

That said there are some basic rules that you need to follow about layout and typefaces.

Table 8.1   Different typefaces

This is a serif typeface	This is a sans-serif typeface
Serif typefaces are based on old printing styles where the serif (the little feet) on the letters allowed the printer to align the metal or wood letters in a straight line before they were inked and printed.	Sans-serif typefaces were designed in the 20th century. The first well known sans-serif face was designed by Eric Gill for the London Underground to be read from a moving train.

Most people find a serif face easier to read than a sans-serif. The eye is guided along the line by the serifs. However, whichever one you choose, don't put too many words on the slide. The slide is not a script – it is there to drive your points home. It may well act as an aide-memoire, but the audience should be unaware of this. As a rule of thumb more than five lines is overburdening the slide. Keep the typeface as large as you can – it must be readable from the back of the presentation room.

For those of you who have never created a slide show, here are the (very) basic instructions for using Powerpoint™. There are many slide show software packages to choose from but they mostly work in a similar way.

■ Go through your script and decide which points need reinforcing with a slide.

■ Open PowerPoint. Choose 'blank presentation', and you will see that a selection of slide layouts comes up. Choose the title page option, the screen tells you where to type in the title and the subtitle, but before you type in anything you need to choose how your slides are going to look. Look at the top of the screen and click on Format, Apply Design Template and you will be offered a list of design templates, click through them until you find one you like and then click Apply. The selected design will appear on your screen with instructions on where to type in the title and subtitle as before. This background will apply to all the slides you create in this slideshow.

■ When you have finished your title slide, click on Insert at the top of the screen and then New Slide and you will be automatically offered the choice of layouts. Choose the one you want for the second slide and off you go. Save your slide show regularly as you create it (File, Save; decide what you are going to call the slide show and where you are going to save it). Every slide show package I have used is easy to learn if you read the screen carefully.

Using presentation software to the full: the power of hyperlinks

The slides you choose for the main presentation can be linked to other slideshows. This gives you the opportunity to go into more depth without having to call up different slide shows if you feel this is necessary – for instance if the audience shows great interest in certain parts of the presentation.

A hyperlink is basically an area of the screen that links the current slide show to another slide show. This can be marked by a visible symbol, (button) or simply a part of the background that has been electronically marked as a hyperlink. To activate the hyperlink the presenter simply clicks on the hyperlink area or button and the next slide that comes up will be from the associated slide show. The related slides also have a hyperlink back to the core show. If the hyperlink area is not activated, the slide show simply goes onto the next slide in the show. This is particularly useful for corporate slideshows, which are typically used by everyone in the company when a 'motherhood and apple pie' presentation is called for, but needs to go into detail about certain departments or products.

I've given an example here of a corporate slideshow for a large IT company. This is used by sales, technical support and management teams. The management team uses the core slides. The sales team uses the core slides, the sales team uses back-up slides (which contain reference sites and quotations from satisfied customers) and the technical team uses the core slides, technical back-up slides and specification slides.

Hyperlinks can also be used to insert video, digital or audio sections into the slideshow.

In most presentation software, it is worth finding out if all the associated slide shows need to be opened before the hyperlinks can be activated.

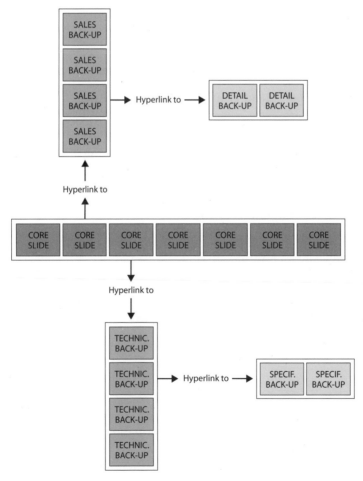

Figure 8.7   Using hyperlinks 1

How to prepare a hyperlinked show

Select the *core slides*

These are the slides that carry the main company message. Before you select them, think carefully about what the audience wants to hear; what are their interests, worries, hot buttons? What is the history of trading between you and them?

■ What is the purpose of the presentation? Keep this in mind throughout.

■ Try to make them visually coherent.

■ Number them.

■ Consider the questions that each slide might raise.

■ If you can link these slides with a theme or a story line, try to do so.

Select the *back-up slides*

These slides prove your arguments: reference sites, case studies, real examples.

■ Again, try to make them visually coherent.

■ Number them.

■ If you can personalize them to fit your audience, do so.

■ Think about what each slide is trying to do – it must add to the sales message.

Select the *reference slides*

These are the slides that go into real detail: although still related to the main message, they contain information that you would not normally show in a general presentation.

Select the *technical back-up slides*

These slides provide the technical information that backs up the main message.

■ Again, try to make them visually coherent.

■ Number them.

■ Try to use slides without too much information on them – keep them simple.

■ Think about what each slide is trying to do – it must add to the sales message.

Select the *technical specification slides*

These are the slides that go into real detail – although still related to the main message, they contain information that you would not normally show in a general presentation, for example, detailed specifications that anoraks will appreciate.

Prepare your slides

■ Prepare your 'contact' slide – this holds the information needed to contact you or the team: name, title, location, phone number, e-mail address.

■ Prepare the 'title' slide.

■ Prepare the 'summary' slide

■ Assemble the slide show, inserting the hyperlinks both to and from the back-up slide sets.

■ Run the spell checker through the slide show and edit it.

■ Rehearse.

Hyperlinks can also be used during the question and answer session where you need to refer to slides you have used during the presentation. Here you can create a slide that stays up while the session is taking place:

NEW TRENDS	THE COMPANY	THE PRODUCTS	THE PEOPLE
THE MARKET	THE COMPETITION	OUR CUSTOMERS	REGULATIONS
REFERENCE SITES	SPECIFICATIONS	COST OF USE	TIME SCALES
APPLICATIONS	EXAMPLES	LOCATIONS	WARRANTIES

Figure 8.8 Using hyperlinks 2

If you have worked out what the questions are likely to be, you can hyper-link related slides to each heading, with hyperlinks on the related slides to bring you back to the question slide.

Adapting information for slide shows

Exercise

Here is a newspaper report on an internet phone.

> The Bisco internet phone. Simple and effective despite inflexible pricing.
>
> This service scored big on simplicity. Once the package arrives, setup involved visiting the supplier's website and registering your details and those of the bundled phone adaptor. With the adaptor connected to the phone and router, we were ready to phone a friend. The tariffs are straightforward but not necessarily genuinely cheap. For instance, 2p a minute is a competitive peak-time rate, but off peak it's pricier than some landlines. Overall the tariffs proved fine value at 4.5 per minute on average and there's no charge for voicemail. Given the emphasis on independence from a computer, the lack of fancy features was no surprise.

If you were selling this phone, what are the main points being made? If you had to put five bullet points of no more than four words each onto a slide what would they be?

When choosing what to put on a slide, go through your script and under-line the important points. Condense down from there.

Although the script from which you take the information for the slideshow may go into detail, the slides are there for the audience.

You need to pick not just the salient points, but choose vivid words to drive the message home to the audience. For example:

▧ simple set-up and registration;

▧ straightforward tariffs;

▧ competitive peak time rate;

▧ voicemail completely free;

▧ independence from a computer.

Exercise

Here's part of a script for a presentation on an MP3 player. Read it through, pick out the salient points and choose five bullet points to put on a slide. The person delivering the presentation is chief salesperson for the XXU10.

Boomaboom XXU10. Great design and excellent sound quality but at a premium price.

This beautifully engineered music machine looks like a modernist walkie-talkie. At either end of the 10-inch wide aluminium enclosure sit two tiny speakers that are driven by a lively built in amplifier. The XXXU10 can be mains powered, or, unusually, from a computer's USB lead. This is simple enough to do, and once connected up plays tunes stored in the computer's hard drive in convincing hi-fi. It easily filled a moderate hotel room but didn't distort even at maximum volume. The XXXU10 made a huge impression with its surprisingly revealing sound. Weighing in at 500 grams it is not especially heavy but the price is fairly hefty. Nevertheless the XXXU10 is a genuine diva that's worth every penny.

Can you think of another way to remind the audience of these features and benefits that would be more interesting than a bullet points slide?

Summary

If we want people to remember what we have said and understand clearly what we are saying then visuals are an invaluable aid. These visuals should harness the imagination, summarize our main points, and make the un-memorizable clear to the audience. They should never be a boring, written repetition of what the speaker is saying. To be sure, they may often act as an aide-memoire to the speaker, but this should be secondary to their useful-ness to the audience.

Keep in mind the limitations of human sight, the boredom threshold of the average listener and the amount of information that the human brain can process at any one time and your visuals will enhance your perform-ance. Over-use them, make them dull or over-complicated, and you will ruin your carefully crafted presentation.

9

Staging the Presentation

In a dramatic production, the stage and the set are an integral part of the performance. A great deal of time is spent designing them and making sure that they both look effective and work well. If only presenters always had a well-designed and efficient platform to present from! In my time I have presented in crowded classrooms, noisy village halls with echoes like the Grand Canyon, in the open air without a microphone and once in a passageway through which the world and his wife passed. I wasn't comfortable and I don't think the audience was either, but there was no choice.

In a perfect world a presentation area needs the following things: space, light, somewhere for your notes, somewhere for the screen and projector if you are using them, cabling control, a place for the microphone if necessary, good acoustics, a non-distracting background, enough distance from the audience to allow you to project your voice without spitting all over the front row, elbow and knee room for each member of the audience, comfortable seats with good sight lines for the audience and an efficient way of entering and leaving the presentation area without having to climb over anything or edge past obstructions. Let's look at each in turn starting with the audience area.

Space

The audience needs enough space for each person to sit comfortably and stretch their legs out, with somewhere to put bags and coats. If you want the audience to take notes or spread handouts in front of them then they will need tables, spaced far enough apart so that no one has to edge round the chairs to sit down. There are several ways that tables can be arranged. Classroom-style means that the audience sit at tables which all face to the front. Café-style means round tables dotted throughout the room.

Conference-style means one large table with the presenter at the head. U-shaped style means a set of tables arranged in a three-sided square with the presenter in the open side. Formal conference halls may have tiered or non-tiered seats facing the stage just like a theatre.

If you have a choice I feel that café-style, conference-style or U-shaped seating is the most comfortable for the audience, as it allows them to interact with their neighbours and have space for papers, water glasses and handouts in front of them. It also allows the presenter to move amongst the audience if needed. Whichever style you have, go round the audience spaces and check that the stage, presenter and screen can be seen and heard from every seat.

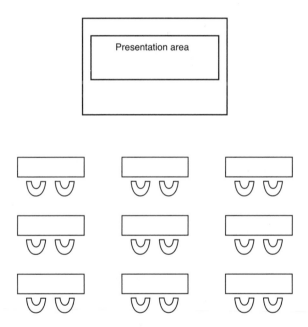

Figure 9.1   Classroom style seating

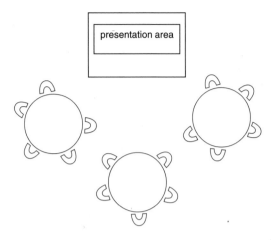

Figure 9.2 Café-style seating

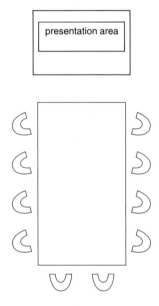

Figure 9.3 Conference-style seating

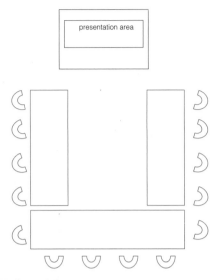

Figure 9.4 U shaped seating

The presentation area

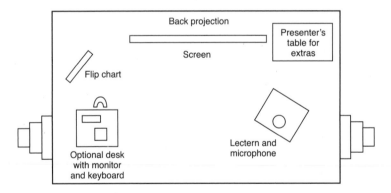

Figure 9.5 The presentation area

The presentation stage

At an absolute minimum you need enough space to take at least five strides from the front to the back and six or seven from side to side. Less than this means that you will feel constrained and your body language will be less convincing. Nowadays, with the sophisticated presentation equipment available, you can have a laptop on the lectern and a small projector at the front of the stage to throw the images up onto a rear screen (be careful not to stand between the projector and the screen if this is the case). Custom-built presentation rooms often have back projection or a fixed ceiling projector, which means you can stride about without worrying about blocking the images. Wherever cables snake across the tables or floor, stick them down with gaffer tape or use a custom-made cable cover.

Lecterns

With the almost universal use of projectors and slides, the lectern has become almost mandatory – it gives you a space for your notes, inbuilt microphone and slide changer and room for a glass of water. The secret to using a lectern well is not to hang onto it like a drowning man but to allow your hand gestures to be upwards and outwards. Whenever possible, come out from behind the lectern and approach the audience, this removes any barriers between you and them and also allows you to highlight important points.

If there is no lectern then you need to have a presenter's table that will take the projector, your notes, water and a glass and any extras. Position this to the side of the stage so that you do not obstruct the screen.

Lighting

When slides were shown in the old days the auditorium needed to be darkened. This is no longer true. Modern screens are luminescent and projectors give such a crisp and bright image that they can be used in daylight. This is a good thing – as a presenter you need to be able to see the audience to gauge their reactions to what you are saying, and of course they need to be able to see you as well as your slides. Beware of any lighting in the room that casts the light up into your face, as it will make you look sinister. Equally, bright spotlights can dazzle you and make you squint, and glint distractingly on jewellery and watch faces. The only problem you might come across is when bright sunlight falls on the screen and makes the image difficult to look at. Check that you can block it out if this happens. Keep the background to the stage and screen as plain as possible – you don't want the audience confused by what they are looking at.

A word about doors. If the presentation room is built expressly for presentations then the doors should be correctly sited, away from the stage; however if you are using an office or a meeting room, try to make the presentation area as far away from the door as possible. You really don't want people popping in and out in front of the stage and distracting the audience. I always carry a 'meeting in progress' sign in my presenter's kitbag that I can stick to the door to deter accidental visitors.

Acoustics

In minimalist modern meeting rooms there may be a problem with resonance. Curtains and carpets deaden sounds whereas shiny surfaces and bare floors cause resonance and echoes. There isn't a great deal you can do with an empty echoing room except to group the audience closer together and reduce the space between the seats and the presentation area. The use of a microphone is very helpful in a fully carpeted and curtained room but sound levels will need to be carefully checked if the room echoes.

There are times when a presentation space needs to provide room for a demonstration. You need to consider the following.

Does the speaker need to be on the same platform as the demonstrator? If so, is the focus on the screen and the speaker? In this case the demonstrator can sit unobtrusively to one side or not even appear on the stage at all. If the focus is on the screen then the demonstrator can also have his or her back to the audience and sit unobtrusively. If the focus is on the demonstrator and the demonstration then the stage must be arranged to cater for this. I once went to an incredible needlework lecture where the speaker demonstrated lace-making techniques. This was filmed by a fixed camera that was focused on the speaker's hands and relayed to the screen. The demonstrator sat at a large table well to the front of the platform so the audience could see what she was doing in general and the detail showed on the screen.

This took considerable organization, and there had to be a break while the stage was set up.

If this is too difficult, it may be worth pre-preparing a video of the demonstration that can be shown while the speaker is explaining what is going on.

Optional extras

Flip charts for a change in pace, flip chart pads and pens, prepared static visuals with somewhere to display them, clock, pointer, laser pointer, extra chair for the speaker, etc.

Summary

A speaker needs to feel comfortable with the presentation area and so should always arrive early enough to organize it the way he or she prefers. Be particularly aware that an audience who feels cramped and crowded will not listen as well as one where participants can relax and stretch their legs out. Equally the speaker needs to feel free to move about the staging area without tripping over kit or edging past obstructions. Take as much control over the staging as you would over a script.

10

Voice and Performance Skills

At last we move on to the presenters themselves and their performance skills. I once had a long talk with the CEO of a very large retail chain that sold all types of entertainment systems and I asked him what irritated people most about faulty sound and vision systems. He told me that people will put up with a poor picture for a while, but that they absolutely hate fuzzy or gappy sound. The same is true with presenters – you can just about get away with a less than professional personal image (though not for long) but you will completely put your audience off if they have difficulty hearing what you are saying. Sadly, when you start a presentation you are likely to be nervous and nerves play havoc with your voice. So you need to prepare your voice before you give a presentation.

The secret of a good voice lies in the way you breathe. The lungs are the power behind the voice and you are going to need all the power of yours to make your voice interesting and audible. Think about tiny babies – their lungs are very small indeed compared with those of an adult, yet when they want to be heard they can make the most enormous noise, without any apparent effort. How do they do this? They use their diaphragms naturally – drawing breath right down to the bottom of their lungs and letting it out without holding back.

Try this for yourself. Stand up straight and consciously relax your shoulders. Place one hand flat on your stomach (just above your waist). Breathe in as deeply as you can.

Can you feel your stomach expand? Has your body become bigger?

If the answer is 'yes', you are well on your way to breathing well; if 'no', you need to practise.

For some reason – perhaps as we learn to articulate words, we start to over-control the way we breathe – instead of drawing breath right down to the bottom of our lungs before we speak, we pull it only half or a quarter of the way down, into the upper chest. For some reason we sometimes hunch our shoulders and draw our stomachs in – all of which are positively bad for our voices. Moving your shoulders up and down makes absolutely no difference to the depth of your breathing – all it does is to make the upper chest and neck area tense and raise the timbre of your voice. Pulling the stomach in is completely counterproductive, since it keeps the diaphragm (the great muscle which controls your breathing) in an unnatural position that actually stops breath getting to the bottom of the lungs. Sadly, breathing like this becomes a habit – and habits are hard to change. The mantra for effective breathing is this: 'breathe in – bigger, breathe out – smaller'.

This is not to say that we are going to take enormous lungfuls of air throughout our presentation, but that we need to learn to breathe much more deeply if we are to modulate our voices interestingly and make ourselves heard.

Here are some exercises to help you to control your breathing successfully. Try them for a week or so and you will feel and hear the difference.

The first step to making a change in a habit is to recognize what you need to change. The first exercise will allow you to tell the difference between diaphragm and 'top-up' breathing.

Try this when you go to bed at night: lie relaxed and flat on the bed (no pillows). Place a book on your chest and a book on your stomach.

With your shoulders and stomach relaxed draw your breath in as deeply as you can, allowing your waist to expand and lift the book on it. Do this several times until you can really feel what you are doing. This is diaphragm breathing.

Now, still lying flat, and with your shoulders and stomach still relaxed, take a much shallower breath, only pulling the air into your upper chest. The book there should move, but the book on your stomach should stay still.

Do this several times until you can really feel what you are doing. This is 'top-up' breathing.

Now alternate the two, taking two diaphragm breaths (book on the stomach moves), then two 'top-up' breaths (book on the chest moves), until you really feel in control.

When you feel confident that you can switch between the two without having to really think hard about it you can move on to the next exercise. This second exercise takes the two types of breathing one step further. Standing up is harder than lying down – you have to use more muscles!

Stand with your feet slightly apart, your shoulders and your stomach relaxed. Try taking some steady deep diaphragm breaths. As you breathe in your belt should get slightly tighter and when you breathe out, slightly looser (if you aren't wearing a belt, tie a ribbon lightly round your waist). Do this six or seven times (no more or you might feel dizzy). Now take six or seven 'top-up' breaths – your belt should feel the same.

Do this three or four times a day until you feel completely in control.

Now that you have the basics of breath control under your belt (so to speak) you can start to experiment. Try the second exercise sitting down, try it walking about, try it with your arms at your side, try it holding a pencil lightly between both hands with your hands at about waist level. Try it using gestures. The second exercise is also useful when you are warming your voice up before a presentation – but more about that later.

Exercise: Relaxing and using your diaphragm correctly

1. Lie on your back with your knees a little apart, pointing at the ceiling. Lie as flat as you can and try to be aware of your back and shoulders spreading – not sinking but s-p-r-e-a-d-i-n-g. Now think of your back lengthening – become aware of your spine and try to feel each vertebra slightly easing away from the other. Allow the head to lengthen out of the back. Shake your wrists gently and let them drop. Move your elbows, feel them become free and let them drop. Turn your head easily from side to side, feeling the muscles free. Press your head gently into the ground, free it and feel the difference between tension and relaxation in the neck muscles.
Say to yourself: back long and wide
Head lengthening out of the back
Shoulders free
Neck free

2. Put the backs of your hands on the bottom part of your rib cage (where you can feel your ribs curving up). Breathe in through the nose, feel the lungs fill with air, and feel the ribs lifting and widening. Sigh out through an open mouth and throat, then push out all the air from the lungs, wait a moment until you feel the need to breathe again, then fill in again slowly and sigh out. Do this two or three times, and then relax.

3. Now repeat the same exercise, breathing in to a count of three – waiting a moment, then breathing out to a silent count of five, then six, increasing the count to ten. Eventually you should be able to count to fifteen and still have some breath left.

Exercise: Breathing fully and controlling the breath

- Repeat the last exercise using the vowels 'AH', 'AY', and 'I', holding on to them longer and making them firmer – then louder, and then return to saying them gently.
- Now repeat the exercises sitting down. A chair without arms is preferable. Try to recall the sensations you felt when you were on the floor. Sit with your bottom well back in the chair to avoid any hollowing of the back. Now relax your head by dropping it forward, pulling it up slowly, feeling the muscles at the back of the neck doing the work. Drop your head back and then lift, drop the head to the side – stretch and lift, now to the other side – stretch and lift, now, drop the head forward and roll it all the way round gently.

  Hold your head in a normal position again, tense it very slightly back, feeling the tension in the muscles at the back of your neck, then free it and feel the difference. This exercise really is the most useful thing you can do to get a sense of freedom.

  To free your shoulders, lift them gently about half an inch then drop them. Do this several times and then just let them sit there – with a feeling of ease.

- Now, to experience the sense of freedom you have achieved you need to actually speak. A few lines from a verse or song will do as long as you feel that sense of ease that we have been striving for.
- Stand up and start speaking the text with your hands behind your head (palms forward, fingertips touching the bone behind the ears), this will help to keep your ribs open. As you speak or sing, gradually bring your hands down. Sing out one part of the text quite loudly on one note, making your breath last out to the end of the phrase – then speak it – conscious of the breath supporting the sound.
- The verse on p86 is an excellent exercise for breath control. Try to say the whole verse in one breath with the ribs expanded – or if you really can't manage that, use the diaphragm at the end of each line. Use this as a warm-up exercise before speaking in public, making sure that you really stress the plosives (Puh, Buh, Tuh, Duh, Kuh, Guh), particularly at the end of words. This will

give your speech crispness. Tape record yourself to see that what may sound exaggerated inside your head only adds a pleasing exactitude to what you are saying when heard by others.

4. Now we are going to use the diaphragm. Keep one hand on the rib cage and put the other on your stomach, just below the waist. Breathe in, filling your ribs, and then give a little sigh and feel the movement of your diaphragm.

The voice itself

Once you have mastered breath control you can move on to voice control. Here we need to consider several things.

Volume, pitch, resonance, articulation, pace, modulation, and phrasing

Volume

As the air leaves your lungs when you breathe out, you have the choice of using your voice box to make sounds, or just letting the air pass out of your lungs, bypassing the voice box.

Try this: open your mouth half way and breathe out without making a sound.

Now open your mouth half way and breathe out saying 'aaaaaaaaaaaaaaaaaaaaaa.' Can you feel your voice box engage?

Now, the way we naturally control our breath comes from how we use our diaphragms, even though we are not normally aware of this – the brain takes care of how much breath we need for long or short sentences – here's an example.

Take a diaphragm breath and let a little breath out between each of the following phrases:

I am
I am in
I am in complete
I am in complete control
I am in complete control of
I am in complete control of the
I am in complete control of the way
I am in complete control of the way I breathe.

You will notice that you didn't have to make any more effort to say the one word phrase than you did to say the ten-word phrase. Volume, however, takes more effort. Provided you have enough air in your lungs, you can alter the volume of your voice significantly. Volume depends on how hard you pass the air through your voice box and how open your mouth is. The trouble is that we hear our voice in our heads as well as through our ears, and all too often we are not aware of how loudly or softly we are speaking. We have to make a conscious effort to speak loudly or quietly.

Try this. Find someone to work with. Count up from one to ten, gradually getting louder and louder, ending up on a shout.

Count down from ten to one, gradually getting softer until you end up on a whisper.

Ask your partner whether you really did get louder and louder gradually or softer and softer gradually. You will probably find at first that these things happened:

■ You didn't get as loud as you thought.

■ The increase or decrease was jerky with the softer sounds suddenly jumping in volume at about six or noticeably falling in volume at about four.

Keep trying until you can raise or lower the volume of your voice smoothly. Many people are truly unaware of how softly spoken they are – particularly when they are nervous about speaking in public. For this reason it is important that you start any presentation loudly – for one thing it catches the audience's attention and makes you sound confident and for another it makes it easier to keep the volume of your presentation at a suitable level (we tend to get softer as we go along if we don't pay attention to projecting our voices).

Pitch

Everyone has their own particular pitch and timbre of voice – the one at which we are most comfortable speaking. This depends on several things – the structure of your body, the tone and pitch of voices that you heard through your childhood, or role models later in life, cultural influences and the state of your health, to name but a few. For example, if you were taught to speak quietly as a child, you may find it difficult to bring volume to your voice as an adult. Some cultures prefer that women should speak quietly and at a higher pitch while other cultures place value on lack of inflection or variation in tone.

Whatever has influenced us often needs to be re-examined when we find ourselves in a situation where we need to address an audience with authority and confidence. Studies carried out in the UK in the early 1900s seem to show that deeper-pitched voices show authority. This does not mean that you have to go about growling into your boots, more that you need to experiment with the natural pitch in your voice and see if you can make it more resonant and authoritative.

Look at the diagrams below. These show how we use pitch to give meaning to our words.

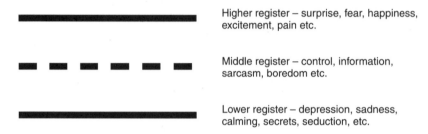

Higher register – surprise, fear, happiness, excitement, pain etc.

Middle register – control, information, sarcasm, boredom etc.

Lower register – depression, sadness, calming, secrets, seduction, etc.

Figure 10.1 Tone and pitch

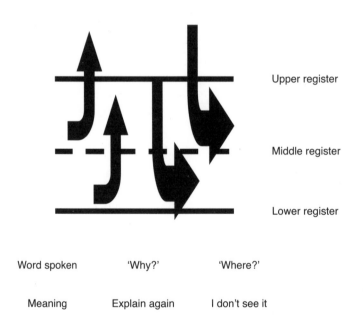

Upper register

Middle register

Lower register

| Word spoken | 'Why?' | 'Where?' |
| Meaning | Explain again | I don't see it |

Figure 10.2 Modulating pitch to enhance meaning

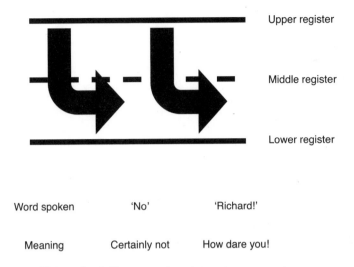

Word spoken	'No'	'Richard!'
Meaning	Certainly not	How dare you!

Figure 10.3 Using the full range of registers in your voice

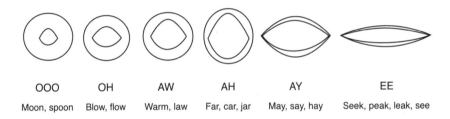

OOO	OH	AW	AH	AY	EE
Moon, spoon	Blow, flow	Warm, law	Far, car, jar	May, say, hay	Seek, peak, leak, see

Figure 10.4 Open vowels

All of us have three main 'registers' to our voices, although we are probably not aware of how much we use them. Allowing our voices to move between these registers gives our words much more meaning than they would have if we spoke in a monotone.

As an exercise, try saying the following sentences in as many different ways as possible. Work in pairs. Each person says each of the sentences in several of the following ways (mix the order up to make the game harder): sadly, happily, angrily, sarcastically, sympathetically, excitedly, seductively, secretively or as if you are bored. The other person has to guess which way you are saying it. Try to over exaggerate the difference between the natural registers in your voice.

Sentence 1: 'If he's not back in the office tomorrow then we'll know what he's been doing.'
Sentence 2: 'Does she think I will believe her?'

Sentence 3: 'Well that's the end of that then.'
Sentence 4: 'No. Really.'

Resonance

If you breathe well, and stand correctly, then it is highly likely that your voice will be resonant. Stance is extremely important in voice production:

This set of exercises, if practised once a day for a few weeks, will improve your breathing, stance, timbre, tone, diction and the flexibility of your voice.

Exercise for posture and breathing

■ Find your 'centre' physically. Stand with the feet slightly apart and flop over at the waist, shake the shoulders, head, arms and hands until loose and floppy, then slowly straighten up the spine vertebra by vertebra until the shoulders and head drop into place naturally.

■ Release any tension in the neck and shoulders, massage the neck and shoulders, roll the head gently around and then lift and drop and lift and drop the shoulders, letting them fall rather than 'placing' them.

■ Stretch your neck and circle your chin in the air, let the chin return to its 'straight ahead' position and feel the space between the base of your ear lobes and your shoulders lengthen.

■ Swing your arms while breathing gently, stretch the arms and spine in all directions.

■ Open the breathing muscles – bear hug yourself and flop over from the waist, then from side to side (this opens the back muscles), put your hands on your ribs and breathe in deeply, feeling your ribs lift and separate (your shoulders should not move while you do this), pull the breath deeply down to your diaphragm keeping your shoulders relaxed. Breathe out on an ssssssss sound (careful with this – don't hyperventilate).

■ Release the lower abdomen. Count out aloud 'one' breathe, 'one, two', breathe 'one, two, three', breathe, 'one, two, three, four' breathe; and so on up to 12 or 15 if you can manage it.

■ Wake up the facial muscles, chew around the jaw, stretch the lips and the tongue, say these sounds fairly quickly:
  – k k k k k k k g g g g g g g g g p p p p p p p t t t t t t t b b b b b b b d d d d d d d.
  – Hum up and down until the voice feels smooth.
  – Count up to 20 using the full range of your voice – exaggerating as you count and try to be really dramatic.

Articulation

No matter how well you breathe or how resonant your voice is, the audience will become restless if you mumble, slur your words or speak sloppily. Not only does badly articulated speech irritate the audience, but also they will be less likely to believe what you are saying. The key to good articulation lies in the way you use your lips, tongue and teeth. This has nothing to do with your accent, just to do with the effort you put into making your speech clear.

The mechanics of speech

English speech consists of 44 sounds.

Twenty vowels:	Do, go, all, further, far, way, seek (long vowels)
	Oo oh aw er ah ay ee
	His, pet, sat, the, mug, on, some, soot (short vowels)
	I e a er uh o u oo
	I, sound, you, voice (dipthongs)
	i ow eu oi
Three nasals	m, n, ng
	my new ring
Twenty consonants	w, y, l, r (semi vowels)
	b, d, g, v, th, z, zh, j (voiced consonants – made with the lips, tongue, palate and teeth *plus* a sound from the voicebox)
	p, t, k, f, th, s, sh, ch (voiceless consonants – made just with the lips, tongue, palate, teeth and the breath)
One aspirate	h

Vowels for music

You will note that the long vowels – oo, oh, aw, er, ah, ay and ee are all made with the lips open and the tongue lying flat on the base of the mouth. This allows the sound to come out of your mouth freely, with no obstructions to stop it. The actual sounds are made by the shape of the lips.

The (open) long vowels are very useful in making your voice musical, indeed the easiest languages to sing in are the ones which have many long vowels. We use the vowels to put music into our voices because it is so easy to vary their pitch.

Look at the first verse of the poem 'Silver' by Walter De la Mere:

Slowly, silently, now the moon
Walks the night in her silver shoon;
This way, and that, she peers, and sees
Silver fruit upon silver trees.

('Shoon' means 'shoes'.) Or think about the way children talk when they are telling you a story ...

There was once a huge monster with great big feet.

Capitalizing on the (open) long vowels will allow you to make your voice expressive and pleasant to the audience. However, musicality is not enough.

Consonants for clarity

If you are working without a microphone – and many presentations require you to do just that – you need to stress your plosives. Plosives are the sounds that burst out of your mouth and wing their way right to the back row of the audience. They are: p(uh), b(uh), t(uh), d(uh), g(uh) and k(uh).

They are formed by opening up the breath behind the lips or teeth or soft palate and then letting it out explosively. These are high-speed sounds and they lend a pleasing crispness to your voice. They are also some of the sounds that people are most careless about. Try saying the following verse really crisply, stressing the start and finish of every word.

DODOS
Dodos died out years ago.
They lived in the Mauritias.
They were eaten up by Portuguese pigs
Who thought they were delicious.

You will find that you had to think carefully about the way you used your lips and tongue. Consonants also use the hundreds of muscles in the lower part of the face, particularly the mouth and cheek muscles. We are some-times very lazy about how we use these muscles; because of this our lips and tongue become lazy and this leads to indistinct speech.

Try these exercises (exaggerate all the movements you need to make these sounds).

Warming up the lips:

Eeeeeeeee oooooooooooooo eeeeeeeeeeeeee ooooooooooooooo eeeeeeee

Mmmmmm ooooooooooooo mmmmmmmmm ooooooooo mmmmm
eee ooww buh eee ooww buh eee ooww buh

tuh buh tuh buh tuh buh tuh buh tuh buh tuh buh tuh buh tuh buh tuh
buh tuh buh

mmmmm aaaah mmmm aaaah mmmmm   aaaaah mmmmm aaaaah
Warming up the tongue and lips:
k   k   k   b   b   b   k   b   k   b   k
la la la la la ma ma ma ma tee tee tee tee puh puh puh puh la la la la la
pit pot pat pet put pit pot pat pet put pit pot pat pet put pit pot pat pet put
pit pot pat
dig dog dag deg dug dig dog dag deg dug dig dog dag deg dug dig dog
dag deg dug
kit kat ket kot kut kit kat ket kot kut kit kat ket kot kut kit kat ket kot kut kit
kat ket
Minimal minimal minimal minimal minimal minimal minimal minimal
minimal
Particular Particular Particular Particular Particular Particular Particular
Particular
Certainty Certainty Certainty Certainty Certainty Certainty Certainty
Certainty
Different Different Different Different Different Different Different
Different
Finally Finally Finally Finally Finally Finally Finally Finally Finally Finally
Finally
Difficulty Difficulty Difficulty Difficulty Difficulty Difficulty Difficulty
Multiply Multiply Multiply Multiply Multiply Multiply Multiply Multiply
Multiply
Impossible Impossible Impossible Impossible Impossible Impossible
Impossible
Yes miss, no miss, yes sir, no sir, Yes miss, no miss, yes sir, no sir,
Clarity of speech Clarity of speech Clarity of speech Clarity of speech
Little bottles, Little bottles, Little bottles, Little bottles, Little bottles, Little
bottles

GORILLAS
Gorilla's legs are plagued with fleas,
They find it hard to catch them.
That's why their hands hang by their knees
It's easier to scratch them.

Articulating the consonants clearly brings another benefit –if you have a
tendency to speak too quickly (and many of us do when we are nervous),
then thinking about how you start and end your words will slow you down
markedly, but not so much that you lose the musicality of your voice.

Phrasing, pause and pace

A phrase is a meaningful group of words that needs to be spoken all in one breath. Most sentences consist of groups of phrases. If we do not use phrasing correctly we make it very difficult for people to understand the meaning of what we are saying.

Look at this sentence:

He was dark black uncombed hair fell over his forehead and down to his collar keys hung from his belt his face was heavily tanned and lined from years of hard drinking he looked dangerous

Without phrasing the sentence is very difficult to understand, but when we phrase it thus, It makes complete sense.:

He was dark; black, uncombed hair fell over his forehead and down to his collar. Keys hung from his belt. His face was heavily tanned and lined from years of hard drinking. He looked dangerous.

One of the main reasons for poor phrasing is lack of breath (but we've fixed that, haven't we!). The other reason is that we often tend to think ahead of what we are actually saying and forget that the whole point of speaking is to communicate our meaning to our audience.

Look through the following verses (which are deliberately unpunctuated) and decide how you are going to phrase them.

> MERMAIDS
> Mermaids may be lovely, with their shining fishy tails
> And their flowing golden tresses and their twinkling silver scales
> But they haven't any morals and they live on sailor's flesh
> (But only when the sailor men are handsome, young and fresh)
>
> YETIS
> On the slopes of Annapurna, when there's nothing going on
> And the climbing season's over and the climbing teams have gone
> Then the Yetis get together and they sing this little song
> 'Let us dance among the snowdrifts let us comb our yellow hair
> Let us frolic round the mountain but be sure to step with care
> For they like to see the footprints that our Yeti feet have made
> (and who cares about the frostbite if it helps the tourist trade)
> For we're the big attraction in Nepal and in Tibet
> And they've never caught a Yeti yet.'

ADELIE PENGUINS
Adelie penguins although sweet have dreadful trouble with their feet they
don't get corns but oh their toes get frozen to the icy floes they love the winter
and the ice and think the Arctic's paradise but dreadful dangers lurk beneath
like killer whales with killer teeth the whales swim round in fearsome packs
and love Adelie penguin snacks that's why before Adelies swim they push
another penguin in and if he sinks without a trace they seek another bathing
place so this is why all penguins say a daily Adelie keeps whales away.

The pauses we make between phrases also help to make sense of what we
are saying. Pauses are also extremely useful when we wish to stress really
important facets of what we are saying.

Exercises to practise pausing and stress

Look at these sentences:

■ It is extremely important that we make no exceptions to this rule.
■ The contract can only be fulfilled if there are no delays of any kind.
■ The most extraordinary thing about this fragrance is that it is
   completely non allergenic.
■ Unless and until this matter is settled we can go no further.
■ Listen to me carefully I shall say this only once.

Where would you put the pauses?

When we want to stress important words we can do it in many ways:

■ We can say them louder.
■ We can say them more softly.
■ We can pause before the really important words.
■ We can say the important words more slowly.
■ We can say the important words more crisply.
■ We can raise our eyebrows.
■ We can make gestures.

Using the same sentences practise with your partner, using the strategies
listed above.

Does my accent matter?

The basic answer to this is *no*! All accents are acceptable – it is the clarity of speech that matters. So long as you can be understood, your accent is just one of the charming personal attributes that makes you what you are.

However – English is a notoriously hard language to speak. (Just listen to some of the regional accents that exist in English – Geordie, Glasgow, Birmingham and Somerset for example, are sometimes quite hard for even native English speakers to understand.)

The English sounds that are most often mispronounced are the following:

- 'th' – as in 'the', 'this', 'that', 'those'. The most common substitution is 'z' ('ze car', 'zis house', 'zat cat', 'zoze horses'), or sometimes by a substitution of 'v' for 'th' ('vis car', 'vis house', 'vat cat', 'vose horses');

- 'th' – as in 'think', 'thought', 'theatre'. The most common substitute here is 'f' ('I fink I know him', 'I fought I saw her', 'we went to the featre'), or sometimes 's' is substituted for the 'th' ('I sink I saw her', 'I sought I saw her', 'we went to the seatre');

- 'w' – as in 'we', 'want', 'watch', 'winter'. The most common substitute is 'v' ('ve are going out', 'I vant to be alone', 'I vatched the film', 'it is vinter');

- 'v' – as in 'very', 'vacant', 'vine', 'visitor'. The most common substitute here is 'w' ('it is werry big', 'the house was wacant', 'the grapes hang on the wine', 'I have a wisitor');

- 've' – as is 'have', 'love', 'give'. Here a 'ff' is substituted ('I haff a cat', 'I luff you', 'giff me the plate');

- the aspirated 'h' – as in 'here', 'home', 'help', 'human'. Here either the 'h' is left off altogether ("ere we are', 'I am at 'ome', "elp me', "uman') or a throaty 'ch' is substituted ('chere we are', 'chelp me', 'chuman');

- 'sh' – as in 'ship', 'shoulder', 'wish', 'shower'. Here 'ch' is substituted ('chip', 'choulder', 'wich', 'chower');

- 'r' – as in 'very', 'river', 'hurry', 'curry'. Here the sound 'l' is substituted ('velly', 'liver', 'hully', 'cully');

- the short 'i' – as in 'little', 'bit', 'miss', 'think', 'bill'. Here 'ee' is substituted ('leetle', 'beet', 'theenk', 'beell');

- 'ng' – as in 'long', 'ring', 'wrong', 'king'. Here 'k' is substituted ('lonk', 'rink', 'wronk', 'kink');

- 'ttle' – as in 'little', 'rattle', 'settle', 'cattle', 'bottle'. Here 'd' is substituted ('liddle', 'raddle', 'seddle', 'caddle', 'boddle') or sometimes the 'tt' is omitted altogether ('li'ul', 'ra'ul', 'se'ul'. 'ca'ul', 'bo'ul');

- the final 'd' – as in 'God', 'hid', 'bad'. Here 't' is sometimes substituted ('got', 'hit', 'bat').

You need to think carefully about the position of the tongue in relation to the lips, teeth and palate when you are speaking. Practise with this paragraph:

I think it is time for a little exercise. I have here three tickets for the theatre that should give us good seats near the front of the stage. James will sit next to Patricia and I will sit next to Veronica. The play we are going to see is *Love's Labours Lost* by Shakespeare. After the play we will go to a restaurant and have a good meal of curry, rice and chips, with many bottles of wine and beer. We will take a taxi home and have an early night.

Summary

We have looked at the mechanics of speech. Here are the major factors that you need to consider.

If you breathe badly this will make your voice less effective. Remember that you need to really fill (but not overfill) your lungs if you are going to make your speech clear. *Breathing in makes you larger, breathing out makes you smaller.*

Tension in the neck and shoulders will show in your voice (it will also make you look nervous). *Relax your shoulders, stand straight and balanced.*

Vowels (the open sounds) make your voice musical. Consonants make your voice crisp. Plosives (p,b,t,d,k,g) make your voice carry. Warm up your tongue and face muscles before you present. *Clearly articulate the ends of your words to make your speech crisp.*

You can make your words more meaningful if you vary the tone and pitch of your voice. Think about the most effective pitch 'patterns' that will make your meaning clear. *Be brave – let the tone of your voice carry the meaning.*

Phrasing keeps the meaning of words in clear groups and highlights the important parts of your message. *Be dramatic – use pauses effectively.*

11

Nerves and Body Language

We all know the feelings we sometimes get before we make a presentation; the butterflies in the stomach, the feeling that we're not totally in control, the dry mouth, the hands that are suddenly too big, the increase in heart-beat, the cold sweat, the trembles. These feelings can sometimes be so over-whelming that they affect the whole presentation or at the very least, the first important minutes. Is there anything that can be done?

Let's first examine what is happening when we get an attack of nerves. We are understandably anxious when faced with the prospect of speaking to an audience, rather than one-to-one. This anxiety is heightened by fear of failing: we worry that the audience will judge us, will find us wanting, we worry that we will forget our words (even though we are the only person in the room who knows exactly what those words will be) and we worry that we will make a fool of ourselves. This is all completely natural, but sadly it can set up a spiral of anxiety. When we are anxious about a situation we secrete adrenalin, the fight or flight hormone, which prepares our body to either stand and fight or run like mad. All very well when in a dangerous situation, but not helpful when we need to look poised and calm.

And what does the body do when preparing to fight or run? The first thing that happens is that we hunch our shoulders and tighten our hands. This is partly defensive and also prepares us in case we need to lash out, (try hitting out with relaxed shoulders – it doesn't work!). Then the adrenalin surge increases our heartbeat, pumping blood to the long muscles in the body in case we need to strike out or run. With our heartbeat increasing, our internal clock begins to race and our sense of timing becomes askew – we take shallow breaths and tighten our shoulders even more. The adrenalin surge also shuts down the bodily systems we do not need for fighting or running, so the digestive system closes down and our mouth becomes dry. Adrenalin also causes our hands to become slightly numb – a good idea if we are going to smite the enemy, but not helpful when we need to make effective gestures. The flight impulse causes us to look away from the enemy (in this case our audience) and look for a way of escape, so we look at anything but the audience and since there is no escape we then tighten our body, often pressing our upper arms against the sides of our torso, or even turning away from all those people looking at us. Indeed, making a presentation is one of the very few times in their lives that most business people have a crowd of people looking at them – except being christened when we are too tiny to worry, or getting married when we have our backs to the audience. Most adults are not used to being the focus of all eyes.

Because this is a strange situation for us, we feel the need for a barrier between ourselves and the threat, so we often fold our arms or hold our notes up against our chest or take refuge behind a lectern, holding onto it like a drowning man. It is a wonder that we don't give the entire presentation from behind the nearest flip chart or video screen. On the other hand the adrenalin surge give us some very positive effects. Our senses of sight and hearing become sharper and our reaction times become quicker.

So, to undo all the negative effects of an adrenalin surge, while keeping hold of the positives, we need to address each effect individually.

Try these actions just before you are due to appear on stage.

■ The shoulder hunch and hand clench: consciously relax your shoulders and straighten your back. Think of the space between your ear lobes and the top of your shoulders expanding. Stand as tall as you can, or if you are sitting, push your bottom to the back of the chair and straighten your spine, try not to hollow your back and push your chest out, this only tightens the chest and will make you sound breathless.

■ Dealing with numb hands and a dry mouth: shake your hands loosely and, if you can, run cold water over the back of them, this cools you down and relaxes your hands and arms. If you don't know what to do with your hands, hold a pen or pencil lightly between them with your hands at about waist height, this causes you to open up the torso and stops you from 'comfort hugging' yourself. Breathe out deeply and then breathe in and out as slowly and calmly as you can. Make sure that you have a glass of water at hand, and if your mouth is really dry, apply colourless lip salve to the inside of your lips which will stop your lips sticking to your teeth.

■ Coping with a fast heartbeat and peculiar sense of time: slow yourself down as much as possible, walk deliberately slowly, make gestures deliberately slowly, speak deliberately slowly, breathe deliberately slowly.

■ Fighting the desire to run away: face the audience head on as you walk slowly into position, look round the audience calmly. If you are worried about looking into the eyes of all the wild beasts out there, looking between their eyes gives the impression that you are looking at them without the alarming prospect of having to make direct eye contact. It is also very useful to have a friend in the audience (within your sightline) who can smile encouragingly at you. Take up as much space as you can – the whole stage is yours to use and if you take up the space and gesture broadly this reduces muscular tension.

■ Before you actually speak, let a little breath out and relax your shoulders again.

■ Stand with your feet slightly apart, as this will balance you and make you look relaxed, and don't worry about the trembles – the audience would have to be very near indeed to notice them.

There are other things that lead to nerves – some of them completely justifiable. Technology (unless it belongs to you) is problematical to say the least. Half an hour spent checking it all out before the presentation is the cure. I personally always carry two sets of any visuals I'm using just in case.

When trying to handle your nerves, remember these rules:

■ Check that all the equipment is working before the audience arrives.
■ Take up as much space as you can.
■ Slow down.
■ Breathe calmly.
■ Don't start talking before you stop walking.
■ Hold a pen or a pencil to give your hands something to do.
■ Always have water handy.
■ Look all round the audience before you start to speak.
■ Learn by heart your first five sentences so you can look at the audience right from the start without having to refer to your notes.
■ Nerves always die out within the first few minutes when you are in control.

Charisma, authority and influence

What is charisma? Webster's New Collegiate Dictionary describes it as 'a personal magic of leadership arousing special popular loyalty for a public figure, a special magnetic charm or appeal.' Look at the television news tonight and decide which people you think show charisma, power, authority and influence. Can you spot any similarities between them, what it is that they have in common? And how quickly did you make your mind up that they had these qualities?

Look out for these things:

- Stance – you will see that no matter how tall or short a charismatic person is, they always hold themselves as if they are tall – no slumping when sitting or standing.

- Eye contact with their audience – it has been noticed by body watchers throughout the ages that high-status, high-charisma people really do look at whoever they are speaking to, using probably 20 per cent more eye contact than the shyer among us.

- Speed of movement, speech, breathing, blinking – this is invariably slower and more measured than in low-charisma people. Have you ever seen the Queen run?

- Gesture – high-charisma people make gestures that are upwards and outwards towards the audience, whereas people who feel insecure tend not to make gestures or if they do, to gesture downwards and inwards as if they are guarding themselves.

Use of space

Space has always been one of the indicators of status – the more powerful the person, the more space they take up; bigger cars, bigger offices, a named car parking space, bigger houses, bigger gardens, and so on. High-powered people are hardly ever crowded by others. President Kennedy said that when he came to the White House as President it was as if there was an invisible line on the carpet in front of this desk that people were wary of crossing. Because of this, powerful people get used to taking up space, even when they are sitting.

Other body language indicates confidence and authority, truthfulness and friendliness.

Teaching ourselves to learn to observe body language is an essential skill for the presenter: not only does it help us to assess the state of the audience, but it also helps us to avoid the pitfalls of negative body language.

Learning to observe

When you start looking at body language, don't try to look for everything at once. Instead, learn the individual components of body language and then put them together.

Start with stance.

Watch how upright people are, including the angle of the head. The straighter they stand the more confident they feel, and the straighter the head, the clearer the thought. Leaning back, or tilting back the head, might infer a need to dominate, leaning forward might suggest interest (or deafness). A sideways tilt might infer interest, relaxation (or too many gins!). Drooping or slumping might infer lack of confidence

What are the shoulders doing? Hunched shoulders imply tension, slumped suggest depression or tiredness, relaxed and straight shoulders point to confidence.

What are the arms doing? Akimbo suggests determination (sometimes aggression), folded might suggest nervousness or disapproval.

What are the hands doing? Clenched hands infer frustration, anger or pain, steepled fingers infer superiority or confidence. Behind the back suggests supreme confidence, and hand on cheek can mean evaluation and interest. The head resting on or being supported by a hand –a sign of boredom or disinterest. Stroking the chin indicates evaluation, and clasping the back of the neck is a danger signal. Both hands behind head can mean arrogance, confidence or superiority. Rubbing or scratching side of neck or ear may be disbelief. Praying hands show a desire to persuade.

What are the legs doing? Standing slightly apart shows confidence and ease. One foot pointing at you shows an interest in you, feet tightly together can mean over-control and lack of confidence. Feet twisted round each other – suggests shyness, displacement activity.

What are the legs doing when the person is sitting? Lightly crossed means confidence and ease. One foot pointing at you shows interest in you, tightly crossed legs mean over-control, lack of confidence, and legs twisted round each other – shyness, or displacement activity. (Displacement activities are the things we engage in when we are distracted, stressed or worried.)

What are the feet doing? Lightly crossed at the ankle, again, means confidence and ease. One foot pointing at you as before shows an interest in you. Tapping denotes irritation or a desire to leave. Toe pulled back (this is the tensor reflex) usually means discomfort or guilt.

What are the arms doing? Folded, self wrapping, shows a need for comfort whereas shoulders shrugged, palms face out shows openness.

Table 11.1 Immediacy and relaxation

IMMEDIACY	RELAXATION
Showing friendliness	Showing ease with the situation
Leaning forwards	Asymmetrical arm positions
Touching	Sideways lean
Nearness	Asymmetrical leg positions
High gaze	Hand relaxation
Direct orientation	Backwards lean
Used towards people we like and by females more than males	Used towards others of lower status, more to females than males, more to opposite than same sex

Proxemics

This is the study of the distances people put between themselves and others. It explains why we sometimes feel crowded, and why it is important to give the audience space when you are presenting.

Approximate distances

Intimate space

Here body contact is easy – we can smell each other and feel their heat, we can whisper, can see each other, but not very well. Intimate space extends from your skin to about the same length as your forearm. It is only used by family, very good friends and people with whom we are intimate. If strangers or people we don't know very well invade this space we become very uncomfortable indeed.

Personal space

We use this for close relationships, we can see each other very well, can touch but cannot smell, can talk easily. It extends from the edge of our intimate space to about another forearm's length.

Social/consultative space is used for more impersonal relationships. It extends from the edge of our personal space to another arm's length. We can still talk, but not so intimately. I call this the cocktail party space because it's the distance that two people stand when holding a glass of wine each.

Public space is anything above the outer edge of the social space. Here the speaker has to raise their voice to be heard. This is the space we present from, if we stood any closer we would alarm the audience.

Signs of stress

In the same way that our body shows that we are nervous, so our body shows stress in several ways: paling, sweating, rapid breathing, sighing and exhaustion, loss of concentration, and sharpened senses/sensitivity to light and noise. We also engage in two types of activities when we are stressed; cut off signals and displacement activities.

Cut off signals

This is what we do when we are receiving too much stimulus (internal and external). We're subconsciously aware that we need to take a break and our body language signals this.

Watch out for these signals – if they occur then it is time to allow a natural break and perhaps encourage the other person to talk so they can discuss their concerns.

Eye signals

- The 'shifty eye': rapid glancing to and fro – almost as if searching for an exit or a more interesting companion.
- The 'stuttering eye': a disconcerting flicker where the eyes can't seem to decide whether to open or close.
- The 'evasive eye': staring sightlessly into the air or downwards.
- The 'stammering eye': a lengthy blink, several seconds longer than usual.
- The 'exasperated roll': a semi-circular movement upwards, usually accompanied by a sigh.
- The 'covered eye': where the hand shields the eyes.

Displacement activities

These occur when people are in a situation where they don't feel in control or are in conflict in some way.

Displacement activities are the body's way of lessening tension. They also occur when there is a conflict between fear and aggression. They also occur when people are forced to wait (another area where control is given up). Watch out for these when you have a waiting room full of people or are at an airport or station:

- intently examining fingernails;
- winding up watches;
- pretending to read;
- yawning;
- foot tapping;
- checking tickets/departure screens over and over again;
- unnecessary grooming.

Creating rapport

When people are in harmony with each other they instinctively mirror each other's behaviours. The closer they match each other, the greater the rapport.

You can encourage a rapport by mirroring your clients' behaviours (not slavishly!). Mirror the stance (both standing, both sitting), their posture, their gestures, their breathing rate, their pitch of voice, if they nod, nod back, and if they smile, smile back. Try to speak at the same speed of voice and keep your blink rate similar.

Eye contact is an important signal. We naturally use gaze as a signal when we are talking. To encourage people to respond, we always look directly at them after asking a question. To encourage people to shut up – when we want to have our say, we often look away from them when they are talking. People look more at people they like than people they dislike. Simply by looking at people more we can make them feel they are liked.

Spot the liar

We can lie with our voices but it's very difficult to lie with our bodies, particularly the feet!

Types of lies

- Expedience – the 'social lie', harmless flattery.
- Necessity – the 'professional lie', used in acting, entertaining, espionage, the law and selling.
- Withholding – playing for time, suppressing negative or hostile reactions in order to maintain the status quo.
- Fear – where telling the truth may lead to punishment.

- Defence – unwillingness to admit to faults in yourself or those dear to you.
- Criminal intent.

Treacherous feet

We learn how to control our face, upper body and hands easily. The further you go away from the face, the nearer you get to the truth. This is why the feet are a dead giveaway for liars. Look out for the following.

Table 11.2 Signs of restlessness

Foot tapping	The tensor reflex
Toes pointing to the exit	Sudden leg or arm crossing
Overcontrolled posture (stiffness, lack of movement)	Extra distance between you and them
Squirming	Hiding the hands
Averting the gaze	Increased head and face touching
Covering the mouth	Flattened tone of voice
Stuttering or slurring	

Putting body language together

Body language can only be interpreted by looking at 'clusters' of behaviours. Try not to rely on just one signal. If the body language is incongruous (i.e. at odds with what is being said) you need to investigate why.

A caveat. Professional liars are extremely hard to spot. They know what the truth should look like and they can mimic it easily – the trouble with professional liars is that they actually believe what they are saying – so it isn't a lie to them!

Summary

Body language is the first language we speak, but we get rusty as we grow up and learn to rely so much on words. Teach yourself to watch the audience for clues from their body language – stance, posture, gesture, facial expression, gaze, position and remember that they will be watching yours.

Are your feet pointing to the door as you read this? If they are it is time I went on to the next chapter.

12

Using Microphones and Autocues

Most presentation venues of any size will provide a microphone. All well and good, but how many of us can remember the first time we used one? Knocking our lips on hand-held microphones, smiting our chests over a lapel microphone and the truly awful feedback screech that happens when you hold a microphone too near to an amplifier.

There is one cardinal rule about using a microphone. You must practise. Even if you are familiar with the actual microphone you are using, you may well be in a different location and every place has its own peculiarities, depending on size, ambient noise, echo, size of the audience, temperature, power and placement of the acoustic speakers, type of lectern and a multitude of other factors affecting the sound that both the microphone and your voice produces.

Most complex sound systems have their own sound engineer. These wizards are an invaluable aid in helping you to get the optimum sound out of the system you are using. Ask for a rehearsal with the engineer and they will set up the microphone and sound levels to suit your voice exactly.

What you need to know before you use a microphone

How do you switch it on and off?

Why you need to know: there may be times during your presentation that you will not need the microphone – then you should switch it off (during a film clip or visiting speaker's session for example). If you don't then any heavy breathing or muttering on your part will be clearly heard. Obviously, you also need to know how to switch it on.

Is it battery powered?

Why you need to know: batteries don't last forever – you need to conserve them when you are not using the mike.

Does it have standby or mute modes – how do you switch between them?

Why you need to know: standby mode is often used when switching between presenters, where the microphone is not in use but doesn't need to be switched off. This is different to an inactive mike. The mute function is useful during question- and-answer sessions.

What are its directional properties?

Why you need to know: there are three types of directional microphones that you are likely to encounter when you are presenting. There are omni directional mikes that will pick up sound from all around them, cardioid mikes which will only pick up sounds from a focused area and hypercardioid, which pick up sound from a highly focused direction. Each one has its uses. The directional quality makes a huge difference to the way you speak into the microphone. Most presenters will be given a cardioid or hypercardioid microphone, so they need to speak across it rather than into it.

Where are the speakers?

Why you need to know: if you are using a hand-held or lapel microphone, you may get a feedback screech if you move close to the speakers. Not a good thing!

How do you adjust the microphone on its stand or fixture?

Why you need to know: you do not want to fumble about if you are following a speaker who is either taller or shorter than yourself and has adjusted the microphone accordingly.

Where is it plugged in?

Why you need to know: if you have finished with the microphone and you don't want the cables on the stage, you need to know where to unplug it.

Once you have mastered the physical workings of the microphone you need to practise the techniques that will get the best out of them.

Types of microphone and how to use them

Hand-held microphones

These are exactly what it says on the tin. You hold them in your hand. They may have a cable that leads to the sound system, or no cable, in which case you will have to wear a radio pack that will relay the sounds to the speakers. This pack is hidden in your clothing, usually clipped to your waistband at the back. Hand-held microphones are usually omni directional or cardioid.

Hold the microphone firmly in whichever hand you are more comfortable with. Check that you have enough cable (where appropriate) to move about the stage, but not so much that you might trip over it. Microphones are extremely sensitive and will pick up any fumblings or clickings you make when you are handling them. Rings can be a problem if they bang against the casing of the microphone. Try not to knock the microphone against anything. Blowing into the mike is extremely irritating to the audience; if you are not sure whether it is working, tap it lightly with a fingernail or say a few words.

Keep the microphone at the same distance from your mouth at all times when you are speaking (typically this is about an outstretched handspan or 15–20 centimetres). If you move the microphone further away your voice will fade and background noises will become louder. Too near and any 'p' and 't' sounds you make will sound like explosions and any sibilants ('sss', 'sssh') become unpleasant to listen to. Hold the mike so that the head is about a palm-width (10 centimetres) under your chin and speak across it, not directly into it.

If the mike is still live and you are not speaking, don't wave it about, but keep it in an upright position and lower it to waist level. Never point the mike towards the speakers or you will get feedback screech.

If you are using a microphone when interviewing another speaker, remember to point the microphone towards the person who is speaking and bring it back to you when it is your turn. One final word of warning, never let the interviewee take over the microphone – you will lose control of it and therefore of your presentation.

Stand microphones and fixed lectern microphones

The same rules apply to using fixed microphones as apply to hand-held microphones in terms of speaking and distance, but because they are fixed people have a tendency to lean towards them and crowd over them. Practise with the sound engineer to find the most comfortable distance to stand or sit, find the right volume and then relax. As before, speak across the microphone and not into it. At your rehearsal, ask a friend to check that the microphone doesn't hide your face from the audience, or isn't in a position where if you make a gesture you might hit it.

Lavalier or lapel microphones

These are tiny microphones that clip onto your lapel or tie so you will need to wear something that has a lapel or wear a tie in the first place. They should be positioned on the outside of your clothing if they are not to pick up every rustle and twitch you make. They may have a wire – so take care that you have, firstly, enough cable to move about if you feel like it and, secondly, that the wire isn't going to tug at your clothing in an ungainly manner. If it has no cable, then wear something that will allow you to clip the transmitter pack on securely or put it in a pocket. Check that the mike is secure as well – you don't want it falling off in the middle of the presentation.

These microphones are best attached a hand span from your mouth. Look straight ahead, put the thumb of one hand on your chin and spread your fingers down your chest. The tip of your little finger will be where the microphone should go. Keep brooches, buttons, tiepins, bracelets and necklaces out of the way of the mike – they make distracting noises if they hit the mike.

Lavalier mikes are directional so turning your head to one side will alter the volume of your voice, so if you have a tendency to turn towards the screen when you are showing slides, it is a good idea to clip the microphone a little more to the right if the screen is on your right, or vice versa.

Typically, lavalier mikes are fiddly to turn on or off, so remember to remove them when they are not needed.

Boundary microphones

These are becoming more and more popular, particularly when a group of people shares the podium. They are mounted on a suitable flat surface and pick up all sounds from all around them. This is particularly good for conferences and round table presentations. The presenter simply speaks as if there is no microphone present. They are often used as stage mikes to pick up all the actor's voices. So far so good, but there is one obvious drawback – when they are on they will pick up everything that is happening on stage, every footfall, tap, rumble and injudicious comment.

In summary: microphones help the presenter hugely if they are correctly used, but if there is no need for them (small groups, beautiful podium acoustics) it is worth doing without. Certainly if the presenter is unfamiliar with them, hasn't had time to practise with them or finds them unduly complicated, they may even have a negative impact. Microphones will not make your voice more musical, modulated or interesting, the presenter must still breathe well, stand well, warm up the voice, use volume, pitch, pause, stress, rhythm and gesture to bring life and interest to what they are saying in order to get their message across successfully.

Autocues

These used to be called *teleprompts* and consisted of a screen with the script scrolling up on it. Nowadays an autocue is a tilted screen or pair of screens, situated in front of the speaker, on which the speaker's notes or script scrolls up. The front of each screen is not visible to the audience although the back is. Often the screen is made of glass and the script is projected onto this, which is supposed to be invisible to the audience.

Double autocues are better than a single one, since the speaker can look from one to the other, which is more natural than staring intently at just one point. Since the type-face on the autocue has to be large in order to read it, only a few lines show at once and as the speaker reads the lines scroll upwards.

> This is what an autocue
>
> script might look like, you
>
> will notice that the lines are
>
> very short and you need to
>
> be careful that your speech
>
> doesn't become chopped up
>
> when you read it.

Figure 12.1 Autocue script

This is disconcerting for the first time user and tends to make speech faster, as if hurrying to keep up with the scrolling rate. There is no need for this, read from the second line down and trust the autocue engineer – if you go slowly, they will go slowly, if you speed up, they will speed up. There are also self-controlled autocues, which the speaker activates with a hand held or foot operated control.

The problem with autocues is that all too often the speaker sounds as though they are reading – and this is very different to speaking from memory. If it is imperative that the speaker must use a defined set of words then it is essential to rehearse with an autocue until it sounds natural.

The autocue can be a lifeline for those people who are worried about forgetting their script. They are widely used at political conferences where the speakers must keep to tight deadlines. With practice, they can be used very successfully, but practice is the watchword – used badly you will sound exactly as if you are reading verbatim and the audience will not believe you as much as they would if you were speaking from memory.

13

Rehearsals

What is a rehearsal for and why is it so important to have at least one rehearsal session before the actual presentation?

Well, when we are thinking about what we are going to say, our thoughts can run at well over 500 words, images and ideas a minute or more, but when we are speaking, even the fastest talkers would have difficulty saying more than 140 to 150 words a minute. It's this difference between our internal thoughts and external speech that makes rehearsals so important.

It is also true to say that until we have spoken our thoughts out loud we don't know whether we can actually say them and whether they will make sense. What happens when we do this for the first time, is that we start to edit what we say as we are saying it, which makes our messages muddled and less authoritative as well as adding in a sprinkling of 'umms' and 'errrs' as we realize that the words newly coming out of our mouths are not exactly what we wanted to say.

There are, of course many other reasons for rehearsals:

■ They let you familiarize yourself with the kit.

■ They allow you to check that your visual aids make sense and are in the right place.

■ You can do an accurate check on your timescales.

■ If you have enlisted the help of a friend you can discuss what questions you might be asked, and then practise the answers.

■ If you are presenting with other speakers, you can help them with what they are going to say and decide how that will affect what you are going to say.

■ They allow you to practise with the person who will introduce you.

■ They help you to conquer nerves.

An effective rehearsal needs to be planned. If you can rehearse in the same space that you will use for the presentation, that's the best. If this isn't possible try to find a space that is similar in size. This allows you to do several things:

- Check out how loudly you need to speak if there are no microphones.
- Work out how you are going to use the stage (will you be trapped behind a podium, can you stride about, where should you stand, where will you put your notes, props, flip chart and so on).
- Work out how to make the best entrance and exit.
- Check out the lighting in the auditorium to see whether the screen is clearly visible to everyone in the audience.
- Find out the sight lines from the audience's point of view (go and sit in a wide range of the seats available and see how well you can see the stage from them).

Now you need to find a rehearsal partner. The ideal partner should know the expected audience and their range of knowledge, business concerns, history, likes and dislikes, and know the issues you will be dealing with. They should be able to:

- Tell you honestly what is good and bad about your performance.
- Come up with suggestions and ideas that will add to the presentation.
- Be as patient as Job and as encouraging as possible.

Collect together the following: all your speaker's notes, a clock or timer, handouts, notepaper and pencils for everyone, feedback sheets, all the kit you will be using, water and glasses for the speakers.

Put aside at least three times the time that you have scheduled for your performance. If you are rehearsing a set of presentations with a chairman and several speakers, you will probably need longer.

Wear what you are going to wear at the presentation. This allows you to check that it works well on the platform. Start by practising your entrance onto the stage. Slow down appreciably both in the speed you walk and the gestures you make. Really look around the audience's chairs before you start to speak. When you are comfortable with this, tell your rehearsal partner why you are giving this presentation and what you want to achieve.

Now run through the whole presentation, using the visual aids you have prepared and being aware of the speed and volume of your words. Your rehearsal partner should make notes on how you are doing with this: a checklist is a good idea.

Table 13.1   General timing rehearsal checklist

Rehearsal Checklist		
Time (Start/end)	Subject (what the speaker is talking about)	Comments (what went well, what went badly, how this can be changed)
Etc	Etc	Etc

Table 13.2   Rehearsal checklist (a)

OVERALL IMPRESSIONS	Good	Fair	Awful
Speed	❑	❑	❑
Volume	❑	❑	❑
Modulation	❑	❑	❑
Gesture	❑	❑	❑
Use of vocabulary	❑	❑	❑
Quality of slides	❑	❑	❑
Organization	❑	❑	❑
Logic	❑	❑	❑
Interest to the audience	❑	❑	❑
Presentation of benefits	❑	❑	❑
Positive start	❑	❑	❑
Powerful ending	❑	❑	❑
Good, concrete examples	❑	❑	❑
Length	❑	❑	❑
Balance between theory and reality	❑	❑	❑
Question handling	❑	❑	❑

Table 13.3   Rehearsal checklist (b)

VOICE	Good	Fair	Awful
Clarity	❑	❑	❑
Modulation	❑	❑	❑
Pace	❑	❑	❑
Strength	❑	❑	❑
Tone	❑	❑	❑
Articulation	❑	❑	❑
Personal mannerisms	❑	❑	❑

Table 13.4   Rehearsal checklist (c)

STANCE AND POSTURE	Good	Fair	Awful
Confidence	❑	❑	❑
Gestures	❑	❑	❑
Eye contact with the audience	❑	❑	❑
Personal appearance	❑	❑	❑
Use of the presentation area	❑	❑	❑

Table 13.5   Rehearsal checklist (d)

VISUAL AIDS	Good	Fair	Awful
Clarity	❑	❑	❑
Interest	❑	❑	❑
Number of slides	❑	❑	❑
Added value	❑	❑	❑
Equipment handling	❑	❑	❑

Now debrief with your partner on how you have done, referring to the checklist where necessary: Did the presentation achieve its objective, and which were the most effective parts? Was it in the right order and what needs changing? Were the start and ending effective?

Rehearse the start and ending again, making whatever changes are necessary. These are the two parts of the presentation where it is vital that you maintain high eye contact with the audience so the more familiar you are with the start and end, the better.

Now you and your rehearsal partner need to look at what questions to expect. These will come in several flavours; the questions you are glad to have and want to answer, the questions you can't or won't answer and the questions you are dreading. Work out the answers and then rehearse them, using the question handling technique of deciding whether you want to answer – if yes, repeat the question, answer the question and only the question, thank the questioner. Also practise deferring answers, refusing to answer and referring to an expert.

When rehearsing with a team of presenters and a chairperson you will need much longer. The sheer stage management of a series of presentations needs to run like clockwork and you need to find out how long it takes to change speakers, rearrange the stage where necessary and for the chairperson to introduce the speakers and to summarize. Remember that what seems a simple changeover may involve a speaker taking the microphone off, the new speaker putting it on, or at the very least adjusting the standing mike – these take much longer than you think and need to be factored into the timetable. Appoint a time-keeper and run through the whole set of presentations without a break.

Add these items to the rehearsal checklist.

Table 13.6   Chairperson's rehearsal checklist

Chairperson's Introduction			
Start time:			
Finish time:			
Presentation 1			
Introduction time:			
Start time:			
Finish time:			
Summary time:			
Presentation 2			
Introduction time:			
Start time:			
Finish time:			
Summary time:			
Presentation 3			
CHAIRED PRESENTATIONS CHECKLIST	Good	Fair	Awful
Chairperson's intro	❏	❏	❏
Chairperson's links	❏	❏	❏
References from speakers to other presentations	❏	❏	❏
Chairperson's closing speech	❏	❏	❏
Overall links	❏	❏	❏
Logical order of presentations	❏	❏	❏
Handling of questions	❏	❏	❏

Have a team debrief after the rehearsal, paying particular attention to how the presentations worked together. Discuss whether they followed a logical flow, if any of the presentations seemed unnecessary and whether they built up into a complete picture. Ideally there should always be time for a rehearsal with a partner, time-consuming though this is. If however this is not possible then you must still practise what you are going to say. Tape recorders and video cameras are invaluable for this so long as you follow the rehearsal rules laid out above. Film your entrance and exit so that you can see your whole body, then film the rest of the rehearsal in medium close up so you can clearly see your facial expressions. If you are still worried about your voice or body language you can try listening back to your rehearsal on voice only (cover up the screen) and vision only (turn the sound down). This is very revealing.

Summary

Without a rehearsal your nerves will be worse, there's a fair chance that you will 'um' and 'ah' when you hear yourself saying your words for the first time, and you won't have a clue how long you will take. No rehearsal means no professionalism – and that's not fair to the audience.

14

Equipment and Visuals

One of the most accomplished presenters I know, Samantha Warner, has the most up-to-date equipment for presentations that I have ever seen. She works for several high-tech companies and so is my source for all technical innovations in the presentation world. I asked her to contribute this chapter.

Clicker/Wireless Pocket Presenter/ Presentation Remote

If you present more than once a year, this is a good investment. A Clicker will free you from the lectern and is a must for anyone using projectors, screens or laptops. They are wonderful devices, which fit snugly in the palm of the hand to give you full control over your presentation. Typically they have forward, back and stop buttons to move slides, bullets, and animations on – much in the same way as the left mouse button would. This is fingertip control; no turning of the head to find a key on a key board, no walking back to click the mouse, no losing valuable thinking time and certainly no 'next slide please, John'. They free you from distraction and allow you to focus on what matters most – your presentation.

My own presentation remote is 'plug and go', with a wireless USB receiver stored inside the remote. When I am about to present, I take the receiver out of the remote and put it in the USB port of the laptop to be used, and it works immediately. The stop button blanks the screen when I want a discussion or switch gears to access another application or file.

Some have bright laser pointers, some have volume control, and some have LED counters to count down the remaining time left. I have worked with software sales engineers who have used their own wireless mice in the same way, but they sometimes get interference depending on the different room environments, the number of people, and so on – when this happens the presentation stalls, they start apologizing, interrupting the flow before finally resorting back to the keyboard. At the time of going to print, I do not recommend using a mouse.

Some other regular presenters I know use their iPod remote controls with their large screen Macs in a meeting room environment, but they switch to a dedicated presentation remote if presenting to a larger group. Perhaps in the future there will be mice that can switch into 'presentation mode'. Until then, a dedicated presentation remote will work through walls and furniture, with radio frequency of up to 50 or 60 feet. My remote has always worked from small meeting rooms to large theatres and in every conceivable machine.

USB flash drive

As a precautionary measure, I always take a copy of my presentation on a flash drive. They are tiny, fit in your wallet, bag or pocket and are there, just in case anything should go wrong with the laptop or it goes astray. They are cheap and can even be picked up at the supermarket. If you do use the drive, transfer it to the hard disk and run the presentation slides from there, otherwise your slideshow may stutter.

Image banks

Type 'image bank' into your search engine in order to find a service. Online image banks are a rich source of stunning images, photography, flash files, video clips and artwork to enhance your presentation. Some of the banks have clever search parameter filters to browse most subject matters (including emotions). You will pay for each download. If you work for an organization with a marketing department, ask them if they have credits with an image bank. A free alternative is the 'images' section of your regular search engine – but check copyright.

Presentation checklist

Pilots use a checklist before every flight. Put everything you need in a checklist and review it prior to every presentation. You will need to add to your own list a section for equipment:

■ projector and power lead;
■ projector bulb;

- presentation remote;
- laptop and power lead;
- power extension lead;
- telephone cable extension;
- plug adaptor (if abroad);
- video adaptor (e.g. DVI to DVI/DVI to VGA) (if projector not your own, check compatibility – is it VGA or DVI?);
- extension cable for modem/wireless modem;
- speaker phone;
- web meeting phone number;
- web meeting audio password;
- web meeting web link;
- web meeting passwords;
- mobile 3G broadband modem;
- portable screen;
- presentation software;
- mind map software.

I have delivered some presentations entirely using mind map software. If you have to deliver complex information and are familiar with the concept of mind maps this is a worthy alternative to slides. Mind maps represent complex information in an organized, easy-to-understand visual format. You can 'play back' your maps to your audience using the playback facility, where you move and cascade through your thoughts like a movie, or you can export your maps to static presentation slides.

In addition, presentations can be launched on the web, linking to web meeting solutions from within the software. Mind map software can easily be found using your search engine, and most offer free downloads for sampling. You can express the 'big picture' in a visual, nonlinear display.

The playback is a powerful visual tool. 'Playing' a map to your audience can enable them to grasp connections and paths easily. Always coming back to a central point to reinforce the core message, you can delve deep into different parts of the map/complex message, without confusing or losing the audience. When coupled with a hard copy of your mind map, your audience will retain more of your message than if you use slides. As with slides, video clips, imagery, icons and graphics can be used throughout the map. This, in short, is a means to present complex information at a glance, so that it is understood.

Presentation software – slides

This section focuses on the capabilities within Microsoft PowerPoint and Apple Keynote. There are other vendors of presentation software and templates.

PowerPoint is not the only presentation software. If you have to present in PowerPoint, you could consider another solution, such as Keynote if you have a Mac, to create the cinema-quality presentations and then simply save it as a PowerPoint file.

Hardware

Factors such as the quality of your graphics card and monitor (or projector) resolution can greatly affect the appearance of your presentation upon playback. Before running your presentation, try the different options to enhance the playback quality.

Close any applications that are not needed to make the most of your computer's RAM and reduce playback errors.

What can be done in a presentation?

Learning how to add and integrate a variety of elements is essential to building a dynamic presentation. Structured tutorial books are available for your chosen presentation software. For now here are a few ideas and capabilities.

You can build presentations that include text, photos, audio and video to inform and entertain your audience. Examples are:

■ Images – photos, illustrations.
■ Video – clips from the news, anything relevant, current and interesting.
■ Animation – text, bullets, graphs.
■ Themes – both packages offer 'out of the box' themes that allow the user to keep consistency in colours and fonts throughout the presentation, including charts, graphs and tables. Beware of using older PowerPoint themes that are overused and appear dated. If in doubt, opt for a classic simple theme. Alternatively a custom theme can help you reinforce your branding and/or message.
■ Speaker notes – dual monitor support with the presentation on the screen and speaker notes on the laptop. Keynote places a timer, speaker notes and next slide info all on one screen.

Keynote

There are usually extra capabilities in Keynote, which began as a software programme for Apple CEO Steve Jobs to use in creating the presentations for Macworld Conference and Expo and other Apple keynote events. Go to http://www.youtube.com and type in 'Macworld' to see one of these presentations. Unlike PowerPoint, Keynote has full support for almost all image types, and the interface and design are much more graphic-oriented, allowing the creation of what advocates of the programme think of as more visually appealing slides.

■ Use 'cinematic transitions' – these are 3D slide transitions, exiting one slide and moving to the next, which resemble rolling cubes or flipping pages, or dissolving transitions that fade one slide into the next. Slides that exit in the conventional way usually feel a bit jarring. These transitions add polish and visual interest and will help set you apart from other speakers.

■ Add animated charts and motion backgrounds to presentations.

After the presentation

Why not put your presentation on the web or DVD? By exporting to a DVD, a PDF file, the Internet or even your iPod, your good ideas and information can be seen by a large audience.

Podcasting

You can create a podcast from your presentation – that is, you can create a small audio file optimized for Internet delivery and synchronize your slides as embedded graphics.

Flash

You can export your presentation to flash, which means that you can create an interactive presentation that is compatible with most web browsers. Flash can be installed on most computers – with such a high installed base this is a good distribution option.

DVD

You might want to publish your presentation to DVD. You can create DVDs to distribute to people who could not attend. You can populate the DVD menu and drop in additional content.

HTML

Placing a presentation on the Internet has several benefits. It allows you to share during the construction stage as well as after a show. It is a good place for attendees to find your notes and can drive customers to your website.

Summary

Presentation technology is constantly being updated – a quick trawl through the Web will make you aware of the myriad of offerings available. Whatever you choose, always allow extra rehearsal time for new equipment and the production of visuals with unfamiliar software.

15

The Question-and-Answer Session

Arguably, the question-and-answer session can make or break a presentation. When the presenter is seen to be speaking 'off script' the audience tends to believe him or her more than during the formal presentation and, of course, the presenter is responding exactly to the audience's specific needs. If, however the presenter is nervous, answers badly, or fails to control the session, then no matter how good the presentation has been the audience will take away a negative impression.

Presenters understandably feel nervous about throwing themselves on the audience's mercy – they worry that they may get difficult questions, they worry that it gives the audience an opportunity to get at them, they feel it may detract from their message or that the audience may try to take over. Indeed, if handled badly it is easy to lose control during question-and-answer sessions. All in all it can be a pretty nerve-racking.

This said, the question-and-answer session does serve several very useful purposes: it allows you to check the audience's understanding – the questions will give you valuable information about what they have or have not understood. It will highlight any concerns from the audience. This is particularly important if you have been giving a sales presentation since it tells you what the customer's hot buttons are. Not only that but it reinforces your message by giving you a chance to repeat the information that is important to them. It is also a vital part of the selling process because it creates rapport with the audience.

This section looks at how to prepare for the question-and-answer session, how to control it, what sort of questions might come up, how to answer effectively, and finally, how to close the question-and-answer session.

Preparing for the question-and-answer session

Up to this point in the presentation the audience has been still – for the most part listening to your voice and looking at the stage area. Now you are going to open the presentation up to the audience so you need to think about the best way to do this.

Moving from the presentation to the question-and-answer session

Having summarized the presentation and given your call to action, now is the time to open the session up to the audience. They have been sitting quietly through the presentation and need a moment or two to adjust. If you move too suddenly into asking them to interact with you the audience will not be prepared and the questions will come slowly. Even the most extrovert of us is often reluctant to be the one to break the silence. However, if you introduce the session carefully you not only keep control of it, but actively motivate the audience to interact.

It is useful to remember that audiences really like the question-and-answer session because it gives them the chance to articulate the new information and explore the subject. It gives them the chance to speak after a long period of silence, a chance to open up the subject and often the chance to show how clever they are.

The secret of a good transition from presentation to interaction is control. When you open up the question-and-answer session you should first lay down the ground rules. These are 'feed forward' controls where you set the limits of the session. You can limit the time ('we have 15 minutes for the question-and-answer session'), you can limit the number of questions ('we have time for three questions'), you can limit the subject matter ('I'll answer questions on the legal aspects of this new contract'), you can limit the questioners ('because we have only a little time, I'll take questions from the human resources department').

You can also exclude certain subjects, ('I cannot answer questions on prices because these have yet to be set'; 'The future plans for this range of machines is still company confidential', 'I cannot make any comments on how we intend to implement this programme since this is our competitive advantage').

Another feed forward control at your disposal is to use a Chairperson. (see Chapter 21). This option should always be used if you have a panel of experts answering questions. The Chairperson allocates the questions to the panellists and if the question is hostile or puts the person who should answer it in a tricky position, can defuse any hostility or even rephrase the question.

A very effective feed forward control is to take written questions only. This takes a little planning (paper and pencils for each member of the audience, helpers to collect the questions and a pause in the proceedings to allow all this to happen) but can be very successful since it allows you to choose exactly which questions you want to answer in front of the audience. As a courtesy to the audience you should answer all the remaining questions after the presentation if necessary.

The final feed forward control is perhaps the most effective. Plant a question with a friend and get them to ask it when you open the question-and-answer session. This means you have another chance to make your main points and the silence that usually follows the invitation to put questions is broken.

Now to actually answering the questions. You need to be very disciplined about this, particularly if the questions you get are the ones you really wanted. There are five steps to answering successfully:

■ Listen carefully all the way through the question.
■ Decide whether you want to answer the question.
■ If you decide you do, repeat and if necessary rephrase the question.
■ Answer the question and only the question.
■ Check that the answer was acceptable.

Listen carefully all the way through the question

This is absolutely vital. Active listening is extremely difficult to do, particularly if what is being said provokes a reaction. Listening is much more complicated than it at first appears. Not only are we dealing with what the speaker is saying, we are also coping with the words inside our heads – and if we react strongly to what is being said then our thoughts can often drown out the speaker.

What happens is this: the questioner starts and we actively listen to the first few words. Then we react and start listening to our internal thoughts – so we don't hear the next few words from the questioner. We then listen again, but usually just to check that the topic hasn't changed. We then go back to our own thoughts and start to formulate our response. When we start listening again we will have missed a great deal of what the questioner is saying, and when the time comes for us to answer, our response is based on less than half of what has been actually said. Active listening means listening as closely as possible without reacting or interrupting.

Here's an exercise to help practise active listening.

Find a partner. Sit back to back and choose one of these topics: 'Six things I hate about my job and why I hate them.' Or 'Six things I love about my job and why I love them.'

The first person begins and the second person listens as carefully as they can. When the first person has finished speaking the listener repeats back as much as they can of what has been said. Then discuss what happened when it was your turn to listen. You will probably come up with some or all of the following:

■ You really wanted to chime in and agree or disagree with what was being said.

■ The more contentious the statement, the harder it was to listen.

■ You started to think about what you were going to say before the speaker had finished.

■ You were easily distracted by your surroundings.

This is what will happen during the question-and-answer session unless you really force yourself to listen carefully. An answer that is based on half a question is only half an answer. Not only do you have to listen non-judgementally to the question, you need also to think what is behind the question. What are they really asking? What seems like a query about the complicated nature of a new software program may be a worry about whether they will be able to master it, and what may seem like a simple question on immediate availability may cover concerns about having to pay up front.

Decide whether you want to answer the question

There is no law written in stone that says you have to answer every single question. You may get questions that you really want to avoid. If you do, you have two options – you can defer the answer and talk to the questioner after the presentation is over, or you can refuse to answer it. If you refuse to answer it is useful to have a few phrases like 'not within the remit of this presentation', or 'company policy doesn't allow ...', or 'I'm not prepared to cover that in this forum ...'.

If you decide you do want to answer, repeat and if necessary rephrase the question.

Repeating the question serves several purposes. Firstly it allows the rest of the audience to hear what the question was (how many times have you been at a presentation where you didn't hear a question because you were either lost in your own thoughts, thinking up your own question or simply couldn't hear the questioner?) Secondly it allows you as the presenter to check that you have heard the question correctly. Thirdly, rephrasing the question may be necessary if it involves technical terms with which the rest of the audience my not be familiar.

Answer the question and only the question. Now is not the time to bring in new topics. What you are aiming for in the question-and-answer session is to expand or explain the information you have already given. Here's an example of what not to do.

A colleague who was an absolute technical expert and also a very good presenter had given an excellent presentation to a group of dealerships about an amazing new computer. When question time came the second question was one that he was really glad to hear: 'Can you tell us when the new computers will be shipped?' He repeated the question and replied: 'Within a fortnight.'

An excellent answer, but then, because he was fascinated by the new computer and loved to share information, added: 'All the awful problems we had with the new operating system have now been ironed out.' This was true but inadvertently he had given the impression that the new computer was problematic – not what he intended at all. So stick to the information that will back up what you have said in the presentation and don't add anything that might have a negative impact.

Check that the answer was acceptable and move on to the next question.

Types of questions to expect

Broadly, questions fall into seven categories: clarifying, technical, anticipatory, peripheral, dilemma, loaded and 'gotcha'.

Clarifying questions

Things like: 'Can you explain …?' 'I'm not sure what you mean by …', 'Does that mean that …?' Are these questions good? Yes they are – they give you a chance to expand your topics and check for understanding. Should you encourage them? Yes. Should you answer them? Certainly.

Technical questions

Things like: 'What is the specification for …?' 'Is X compatible with Y?' Or: 'If the subflammary injection sprinzer is calibrated with the pulmintary inhibitation valve what happens to the misgenic saving counter and the vertical scat mitigator and the …?' Are these questions good? Yes and no. Should you encourage them? Yes and no. Should you answer them? Eventually, yes, but you need to think this through. If the audience is predominantly technical and if you can keep the answers short, by all means answer them, but if the audience is not particularly technical and you know full well that the technical specification will not be remembered then have the information in a hand-out and refer them to it.

And what about the third type of technical question? What is happening here? It may well be a genuine query but often it is simply an effort on the part of the questioner to prove just how much they know about the subject. If you feel this is the case, thank the questioner and defer the answer until after the presentation is over.

Anticipatory questions

Things like: 'Will you be talking about …?' or 'What about xxx (the subject of the next presentation)?' or 'Will you be covering …?' Are these questions good? They certainly are. Should you encourage them? Yes indeed. Should you answer them? Yes, but not with an actual answer about the topic.

When you go to the cinema there is usually a series of 'trailers' for forthcoming attractions; these whet your appetite and are supposed to make you come to see next week's films. Anticipatory questions do exactly the same thing. They give you a chance to connect with the audience when you do introduce the topic and you can then personalize it by saying something along the lines of 'This next topic is the one you were interested in Mr Brown.' So causing him and indeed anyone else who wanted to know about it, to sit up and pay attention.

Peripheral questions

Things like: 'When I was in India …', 'I had a very interesting experience when …', 'In my experience blah blah blah …', 'My field of expertise tells me …'. Are these good? It depends. Should you encourage them? Maybe. Should you answer them? Answer what? These are probably not questions at all. Here you need to think about what is actually going on.

If you have invited the audience to share their experiences then they are an excellent way of creating rapport and you should welcome them – they give the audience a chance to match up what they know to what you have just presented to them. If however, time is tight and you know that other questions are waiting you need to tactfully get the questioner to move on.

That said, you also need to think about the questioner's role in the audience. If you have made a selling presentation and the person sharing their valuable experience with everyone happens to be the one who will sign the contract, then it may be politic to listen raptly and thank them profusely when they (eventually) finish.

Dilemma questions

These are questions that put you in a real spot – such as requiring company sensitive, pricing or competitive information that shouldn't be aired publicly. Are these good? Yes and no. Should you encourage them? Yes and no. Should you answer them? Not in public. If you are prepared to share the information required then do it off line – not in front of the audience. If you can't, then tell the questioner so and don't answer.

Loaded questions

These questions are often used where the questioner obviously has a sub-agenda and is waiting for you to step right into it. Often, a question seeded by your competitors. Are these good? That depends. Should you encourage them? Again, that depends. Should you answer them? Hmmm.

Loaded questions may be uncomfortable but they do give you the opportunity to correct misinformation and set the record straight. It is worth rephrasing these questions if you are going to answer them. Turn the question from negative to positive and answer crisply and succinctly. Don't be pulled into an argument, keep your body language and voice positive. When you have finished your answer, look away from the questioner and ask for another question from the rest of the audience.

'Gotcha!' questions

These are malicious or unanswerable questions that are a mixture of dilemma and loaded questions and they are always asked for negative reasons. Are they good? Certainly not. Should you encourage them? Never (but if you can find out before the presentation whether there is anyone in the audience sharpening up their sword and loading the machine gun, you are at least forewarned). Should you answer them? No. Be uncompromising, refuse to answer, don't look at the questioner, don't get into an argument and try not to be affected by them. By the way, unless you have been saying extraordinary things or have a murky past, 'Gotcha!' questions are mercifully rare.

Exercise

Go through your presentation and think about the questions that you might be asked. Make one question a clarifying one, one a loaded or 'Gotcha!' and one that might need to be deferred.

Tracking the question-and-answer session

As soon as possible after the presentations, fill in a question-and-answer tracking form. This not only keeps a note of who was interested in what but also ensures that any deferred questions are handled quickly

Table 15.1 Question tracking

Questioner	Question	Answer	Comments	Sent?
John Smith Cameron-Smith Ltd. UK	What is the price break on orders of more than 100?	(Deferred until after the presentations) 100–150: 10% off 150–200: 12% off 200 and over, negotiable	His company always buys in bulk. He's ready to order	E-mail 1/12/08
Phil Barnum Philindustries UK	What range of colours is the MX30 available in?	(Answered at the presentation) Red and blue only	He wants customized MX30s and is prepared to pay	Follow up with visit

The question-and-answer session, if successful, is an absolute goldmine of information for the presenter. You need to make a note of the questions asked and hold a 'wash-up' session after the presentation is over. Look through the questions – do they show a trend? Which questions did you have difficulty in answering? Do you need to get information to the questioners? If you deferred questions, have you handled them now?

Summary

The question-and-answer session gives you a wonderful chance to really reinforce your messages and get close to the audience. It is not, however a time to sigh with relief that the body of the presentation is over. Q and A sessions need just as much self-control as delivering the presentation. You would be surprised how difficult it is to remember to even repeat the questions that you want to answer in the hurly-burly of this session. You also need to keep complete control over the audience using feed forward controls. Handle the question-and-answer session well and you will have the audience firmly on your side at the end of the presentation.

16

Delivering the Presentation

Here we are at last. We've considered the audience, their interests, needs and behaviours and they know what to expect. We've prepared the script and know what we want to talk about and the limits on this. We've prepared the visuals and back up materials. The stage is perfect, all the kit is in place. We've thought about the questions that might be asked. We've rehearsed and warmed up our voice and our nerves are not overwhelming us. So – best foot forward and off we go.

First impressions

A great deal of analysis has been done about what makes some people credible and charismatic and others less so. There are two sides to this; what the audience believes and what the audience sees.

Credibility – what the audience believes

Are you reliable, dependable, predictable and consistent as an information source? Are you an expert on the topic under discussion? Do you and your company have a reputation for accuracy and truthfulness? What are your motives? Are you being open about the effect you want to have on the audience?

If you have a chairman or master of ceremonies, they can introduce you and make the credibility statement for you – if not, you need to do it yourself. This should come near to the start of the presentation. However, before you even open your mouth, the audience will have made up its minds about you, so let's have a look at what charisma and credibility look like.

The audience will start to decide whether you are believable from the moment they set eyes on you – even though you may not be speaking.

Take this scenario: the stage is set, there are chairs on one side where three presenters are sitting. The chairman is at the lectern and introduces the first speaker as one of the world's leading experts on the spread of bovine tuberculosis, the author of seven books on the subject, the leader of a task force working for the Ministry of Agriculture, broadcaster and pundit and owner of one of the largest milk herds in the South of England.

This presenter is nervous, sitting slumped on his chair, fiddling with his notes. As the audience's eyes swivel across to him he visibly starts, gathers his notes together, dropping several of them. He gets out of his chair and scuttles across to the lectern, shoulders hunched, eyes resolutely away from the audience. Just before he reaches the lectern he starts to speak in a low, rapid and breathless voice, eyes still resolutely away from the audience. He launches straight into his presentation, but the audience can't hear him because he isn't speaking into the lectern microphone – he's desperately clutching the sides of the lectern and reading from the screen where the first, amazingly complex slide is showing. As he speaks, his nervousness begins to fade, his voice gets stronger, he looks at the audience (noticing that they are chatting amongst themselves and reading their handouts, several of them with their arms folded across their chests), he releases the lectern from his iron grip, and makes an expansive gesture, his voice becomes interesting, he stops reading from the screen and launches into an amusing and apposite example …

Sadly this is all too late. The audience's interest is lost.

Exercise

Make a list if the things he did wrong. What could he have done instead?

Exercise

Over the next few days, identify charisma and credibility in the people you meet or see on the television, particularly on the news. Look at the way they stand, sit, walk, gesture and interact with others. What do they all have in common? You will find that they usually fit all the factors in the charisma recipe.

The charisma recipe

The 4 Ss

■ Stance – stand tall with a straight back. No hunching, twisting, hiding of the body behind folded arms or your notes. Keep your shoulders level and relaxed. The space between your ear lobes and your shoulders should be as great as possible without lifting your chin.

■ Sight – really keep your audience in sight – we all instinctively know the difference between staring and good eye contact. Unless you look at the people you are talking to they will not believe you.

■ Speed – slow down, slow your breathing, walking and gestures.

■ Space – take up as much space as you can, don't keep your arms close by your sides, instead, clasp your hands loosely at waist level if you feel nervous. Make your gestures wide, upward and outward. An entrance like this will give you great credibility.

Don't start talking until you've stopped walking. Take your time getting into position, look round your audience and smile (not an inane grin but a genuine smile).

If you are speaking to a huge audience you cannot possibly make eye contact with all of them but you can give the appearance of doing so. Here is how.

Imagine that a huge figure 5 is suspended at head level over the audience with the top across the back row, the side halfway down the left hand side and the curve over the rest of the audience:

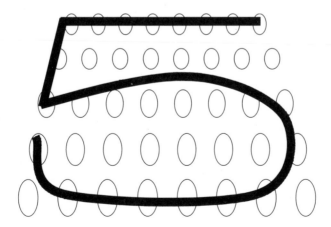

Figure 16.1   Looking at the audience

Slowly look at this figure 5 moving your eyes and head. As you come to the final part of the curve your chin comes up and the audience will know you are going to start. They will also believe that you have looked at each and every one of them.

Being well rehearsed, you will be able to start your presentation off without referring to your notes. Make sure that you are loud enough – it is easier to start at a higher volume and drop your voice if necessary than it is to start too softly and try to raise the volume later. It's the same with gabbling – if you start too fast it is hard to slow down later.

Let your enthusiasm show. Audiences respond very positively to enthusiastic presenters who also show warmth and friendliness.

Are you dynamic enough? Dynamism and emphatic speech are seen as more credible.

If you clearly 'own' your message by using personal pronouns ('I', 'my', 'we', and not 'most people', 'some of our friends' etc.) you will have the audience on your side, right from the start.

Starting with a bang

One of the most effective presenters I have ever seen had an amusing gimmick. When he came onto the stage he carried with him the most enormous bottle of water. He placed it carefully on the podium and never referred to it during his presentation. When he came to the question and answer session he broke the ice by saying 'I bet one or two of you are wondering what's the significance of this enormous bottle. Well, I sometimes get nervous at the start of a presentation so if I bring this bottle on with me, the audience looks at the bottle for the first few moments and not at me – which helps my nerves no end.' He was a very amusing presenter and had a very light touch so he got away with it.

Now you may not need to bring an enormous bottle of water with you, but you do need to start with a bang (particularly if you have drawn the short straw of the post lunchtime slot). You need to make the audience sit up and look forward to your presentation. Here are some of the things you could do.

Start in a conversational tone with an anecdote that exactly illustrates what you are going to talk about. This creates rapport with the audience before you start into the facts and evidence.

Find a piece of music or a song that really fits with the presentation subject or theme and have it playing while you make your entrance. You can then start by referring to the song and why it is relevant. I use a Pete Atkins song 'The Master of the Revels' when I'm making a presentation about presentation skills.

Start by asking the audience a question, and making sure that they know you really would like an answer.

Single out a member or section of the audience that you had researched before the presentation and talk about them, making sure you use their names and their company name: this really makes them sit up.

Another magnificent sales presenter I know is skilled at simple magic and often starts his presentation with a trick that involves filling a seemingly empty container with vast amounts of (probably fake) £5 notes. He then asks the audience if they would like to do this for real and segues into his speech from there. Whatever you do you need to think about the first impression you are going to make and not just launch straight into the presentation.

Keeping the pace going: once you have overcome any nerves and started to relax into the presentation, you need to keep the pace up. If you are breathing well and standing properly you should have no problem but in hot presentation venues it is surprisingly easy to find your voice and energy flagging. These are the things to watch out for:

■ Dropping your voice at the end of sentences. This happens because you are so busy thinking about what you want to say next that you allow your voice to tail off before you have finished talking. Remember that although you may be thinking ahead, all the audience can hear is what you are actually saying.

■ Speeding up. This happens because you really want to get all your points across. Force yourself to speak more slowly by stressing the plosives (P, B, T, D, K and G) at the start and ends of your words. This not only slows you down, it also makes you easier to hear.

■ Starting to talk before the audience has had time to read, look at and understand the slides. Make yourself introduce every slide carefully.

■ Concentrating so much on what you are saying and what is on the slide that you stop looking at the audience. This is deadly. You really need to know how the audience is responding to you, your body language watching skills need to be really honed during a presentation. To focus on the audience again you could ask them a question, or throw out something controversial (as long as this doesn't interrupt your main message), and see what happens.

Keeping to time: if you find that the audience is very lively and are showing signs of great interest (sitting straighter, leaning forwards, smiling and nodding), then asking them what particularly interests them about that particular section of the presentation is a good idea. However this can play havoc with your timing, and if you are part of a series of presentations, this is not fair for the other presenters. If this happens, you may have to cut down on some of the information that comes later in your script. The audience will never notice and you can always pick up these points after the presentation or in the question and answer session.

Keeping to the script: you are the only person who really knows what is in your script. A presentation is not a performance of an opera where the audience may know all the songs; so long as you cover the main points adequately this will be enough.

This brings me on to responding to the audience's response – I mentioned earlier that if you spot great interest in what you are saying you can get the audience to tell you why – well, this cuts the other way too. If you see the audience nodding off (and I assure you that one day this will happen – I nearly fell asleep at 2.15 in a presentation and I was one of the speakers), you need to make a change of pace and focus. Asking the audience a direct question (and waiting for the answer), or asking the audience to share experiences with you, will re-energize them and make them listen again.

Your final bow

You're on the home straight, the questions have been answered as far as is possible, you have made a rousing summary and a dynamic call to action, pitching your voice up and injecting energy and enthusiasm into it, and now you have to leave the stage. Do not scuttle away. Come out from behind the lectern if you have been delivering from there, move to the front of the stage and finish with a big gesture towards the audience. At this point, if you have done a brilliant job, you will probably get a round of applause. Accept it! The British are usually bashful about applause, but you really do deserve it and you should enjoy it.

When it dies away, thank the audience for their attention if you think this is suitable, thank any other speakers if necessary and try to find a way to move into the audience if you can. Handouts are an excellent excuse for this, have four or five available and go down to the front row and hand them out, pointing out before you do that they are available for all the audience (tell them where the handouts are, of course).

Summary

You need to keep your energy and enthusiasm high throughout the presentation, rising to a splendid finish. Don't hurry the start or finish – these are the parts of the presentation that will be remembered the most. And enjoy your applause.

17

Technical Presentations and Demonstrations

Technical presentations

tech·ni·cal adj a: having special and usu. practical knowledge esp. of a mechanical or scientific subject. **b**: of or relating to a particular subject esp: a practical subject organized on scientific principles.

Technical presentations give rise to several particular challenges:

- Technical language (jargon). In most presentations, jargon should be assiduously avoided; however, in technical sessions the users must become familiar with the technical terms needed in order to ask other specialists for advice, fault reporting to manufacturers and indeed talking to other specialists in a language that they all understand.

- Fairly rigid procedures. There are always several ways of using technology – however some are more efficient than others and these are the ones that need to be shared with your audience.

- Fear. New users of technology are terrified of it – they are afraid of failing, afraid of looking stupid, afraid of damaging something, or afraid that they will lose their old skills.

- Necessary background knowledge. It is important for the user to understand the basic principles behind the technology, or the learning is only 'parrot fashion', and useless in a situation where a mistake needs rectifying.

- Safety and legal procedures. There is often a need to know about and perform several procedures that are time-consuming and not particularly interesting (backing up computer disks for instance, or telling the audience where the fire exits are). Making people realize the importance of these is difficult, since most of us would prefer not to undertake the extra effort they require.

So, how to overcome these potential problems?

Sound knowledge on the part of the demonstrator.

You must know your stuff, and understand it fully. Preparation is the key here. When learning new technologies yourself, keep a notebook by you and note down which things you found the hardest – these are the very things your trainees will find difficult, and where you will need to spend extra time on the course. A section in your presentation entitled 'Technical Language. A Glossary of Terms' is essential – put the main technical terms up on a large flip chart, with their meanings.

Run a little quiz at the beginning of each session.

Whenever you need to introduce a new term, give a full explanation of it and reinforce this several times. It is amazing how many technical terms we use as if they were familiar to the entire world.

Necessary background knowledge

How is the equipment plugged in? How do you switch it on? What connects to what? What if there's a power failure? What can I touch? How do you switch it off? How do you disconnect it? Is it breakable? How do I keep it clean? Where is the information stored? If I don't type it in, where has it come from? Is there anything I have to do each day – at the beginning? At the end? Who can I contact when it goes wrong? When I go wrong? Where is the information stored? Is there a manual? How do I use it?

Make a list of all the basic facts that the users really must know and all the facts that would make the users feel more comfortable. Put it in the handout, pin it on the wall, tell them about it! Ignorance is *not bliss*, ignorance is frightening (particularly to a new user) – anything you can do to reassure them will make your job as a trainer easier. The pure theory behind technology should be left alone in the main – after all we don't need to know about the physics of water pressure and rotation to be able to use a washing machine, but we do need to know where to switch it off should a flood occur!

dem·on·strate vt 1: to show clearly; **2a:** to prove or make clear by reasoning or evidence; **2b:** to illustrate or explain esp. with many examples; **3:** to show or prove the value or efficiency of to a prospective buyer.

This is particularly useful when showing a group/person how to use new technology.

A good demonstration should serve these purposes:

- to show visually how things link together;
- to simplify what may at first seem complicated;
- to show cause and effect;
- to explain what sequence of events is needed to use the product;
- to allay any doubts or worries about the product;
- to encourage the group/person to use the product;
- to discover the user's needs in detail;
- to show the most efficient way of using the product;
- to show the capabilities of the product.

There are basically three types of demonstration: the performance demo or 'watch my magic fingers', the interactive demo or 'what would you like to see next?' and the teaching demo where you pass your expertise on.

The performance demo

This is where the accomplished operator sits down at the technology and gives a virtuoso rendition of that old favourite – 'I'm doing this so fast that no one can tell what I'm up to but my goodness – the results look impressive!'

There is no place for this in a presentation. It scares the daylights out of the inexperienced and makes the kit look difficult to use. It communicates absolutely nothing.

The teaching demo

This is an excellent selling tool as long as these simple rules are followed:

- Introduce the demo very clearly: 'What I am going to show you is ... this will be useful to you when you need to do ...'
- Do not attempt to do too much but try to link the new skills to existing skills: 'Now that we know how to log into the system we are going to create a file to work in ...'

Say what you are going to do then do it slowly. Recap on what you did. Don't take any short cuts. New users need to know how to do things correctly the first time they try – they can work out their own short cuts later when they are familiar with the kit. This is particularly true when you are demonstrating any machinery that is potentially dangerous.

- Explain all technical terms in plain English.
- Make sure you can be seen and heard.
- Don't hurry, but don't take too long – the trainees will want to try it for themselves.

The interactive demo

Here, the user and the demonstrator sit and work together. This is an excellent tool both to introduce new skills and to help cure any faulty skills. The secret of a good interactive demo is to allow the user to do most of the talking, only joining in to explain or set tasks. Here's how to do it:

- Find out from the audience what they need to learn.
- Find out how much they already know (you can do this by asking them to show you a particular technique).
- Set a new task, explaining clearly why they need to know this and what the outcome will be.
- If there is no way that the trainee can work out the new task, then demonstrate slowly, using teaching demo techniques.
- Ask the user to try it – at least twice. Get them to explain what they did. If they make a persistent mistake, show them again using positive reinforcement.
- Move onto the next task, linking it to the one just learned.
- Keep an eye on the time – don't let them work for more than 20 minutes without a break
- At the end of the session, ask them to tell you what they have learned.
- Praise when they do well – but be specific.

Setting demonstration objectives

Just as there needs to be a set of objectives for a presentation, there needs to be the same for a demonstration.

The objectives for the demonstration itself

- to persuade the audience to buy your product;
- to update the audience on progress in a project;

- to train the audience to use a piece of equipment;
- to make a case for a project or business case.

The audience's objectives

- to decide whether to buy or not;
- to hear how things are progressing;
- to learn how to use a piece of equipment;
- to decide on a course of action.

The demonstrator's objectives

- to further the business relationship with a client;
- to prove how efficiently you have carried out your job;
- to help your team use new equipment;
- to get your proposal accepted.

And they must pass the SMART test:

- Can it be *Simply* expressed in one sentence?
- Do you know how you will *Measure* the success?
- Is it *Achievable* – has anything like this been done before?
- Is it *Reasonable* allowing for the resources you will need?
- Is there a *Timetable* for this?

Write down objectives for the next demonstration you are going to give:

- demonstration title;
- demonstration objectives;
- audience objectives;
- personal objectives.

Here is an assessment exercise for the need for a demonstration as opposed to any other presentation method:

1. Does this information need to be shown to more than three people at once?
2. Is this information that needs to be explained carefully and at length?
3. Is this new information to the audience?
4. Does this information need to be presented in the same way to a number of different groups?

5. Does the proposed audience really need this information?
6. Can I afford the time to prepare this demonstration?
7. Can the audience afford the travelling time for this demonstration?
8. Is this information completely up to date?
9. Do I have a room and the equipment for this demonstration?
10. Do I know what the audience wants from this demonstration?
11. Will this demonstration be cost effective?
12. Have I given the audience enough warning of this demonstration?

If you answer yes to questions 1 and 2, and to most of the rest of the questions, you have a good reason to give the demonstration.

If you score no to questions 2,3,5 and 8, then you need to research your subject more carefully before you give the demonstration.

If you score no to questions 1,6,7,9 and 12 you need to look at logistics carefully.

If you score no to questions 1 and 11 you should look for another way to get the information across.

Preparation checklist for a demonstration

■   What do you need to include on your title slide?
–   Presentation title
–   Presenter's name
–   Contact details for presenter
–   Client's name
–   Client's logo
–   Theme statement
■   What do you want the audience to do with the information you are presenting?
■   What must you include to help the audience to do this?

Let's look at the differences between presentations and demonstrations.

Table 17.1 Presentations vs demonstrations

● PRESENTATIONS	● DEMONSTRATIONS
● Presentations need a clear and compelling start	● Likewise
● Presentations need a clear and compelling end	● Likewise
● Presentations link new information to old	● Some demos show entirely new stuff
● You can always see the presenter	● You can't always see the demonstrator
● The presenter is the focus of a presentation	● The demo is the focus, not the demonstrator
● The audience can interrupt a presentation if they need to	● Most complicated demos have a fixed time and pattern
● The presenter needs to concentrate on only their words and the audience	● The demonstrator needs to concentrate on words, audience AND the kit.
● Any visuals back up the presenter's words	● The demonstrator's voice backs up the demonstration
● If the equipment breaks down it's under the presenter's control	● If the kit breaks down you may need help
● The presenter can see the audience's reactions	● The demonstrator must concentrate on the kit
● The presenter can move about	● You are tied to your kit!
● The volume of most presentations is based on the presenter's voice	● The demo may be so loud that your voice will sound weak in comparison
● Only a few presentations need a change in the ambient light	● Some demos need to have the lights lowered
● Presenters usually know a great deal about their audiences	● Sometimes you don't know who is in the audience until it's too late
● A presentation is always tuned finely to audience needs	● It *should* be the same
● Most presenters feel comfortable with what they are saying	● A demonstrator may be comfortable with the kit and the demo but a little unsure about the business issues

Demonstrations

Demonstrations need a clear and compelling start. What are they going to see/hear? Why are you showing them this? What will fascinate them? What will amaze them? What questions will the demonstration raise in their minds? Use the start of the demonstration to tell them all this – prepare them and put them into a state of active looking and listening.

Demonstrations need a clear and compelling end. Try to end on something that will show them that what you are demonstrating can do something for their business.

Some demos show entirely new stuff. When we see or hear something that is new to us we try to make sense of it by relating it to something we have already experienced – because of this a good presenter should link new information with existing information. However, in the case of a splendid demonstration, your audience may never have seen anything so extraordinary, and they will have nothing to compare it with. Also, the audience may well be so amazed with what they are seeing that they may need reminding of the strong business purpose behind what they are experiencing.

The audience can't always see the demonstrator. This is a difficult one. You may be running the demonstration from the back seat – they can't even see your head, let alone your legs! Now, at least 60 per cent of the meaning of what you say is communicated by your facial expression, gestures and stance – and you don't have any of those visible to the audience. You will have to use vocal emphasis to fill in the gaps. Use pause, volume, pace, speed and inflection to make your voice more dynamic. The demo is the focus, not the demonstrator – and you may be at the back! By the way, it isn't true that you can't hear a smile – you can!

How many conversations do you have with the back of someone's head? As above, you'll have to make your voice do all the work. However, you still need to show the audience your legs (as it were) so introduce yourself to them in the presentation part of the demo. If you are doing a two-handed demo/presentation you should still make sure that the demonstrator is introduced, and that the demonstrator joins in the presentation and question-and-answer part of the demo as well.

Most complicated demos have a fixed time and pattern. This can be limiting if you are trying to persuade or make a sale, when you want as much input from the audience as possible. If you can build in pauses and natural breaks into the demo, these will give the audience a chance to ask questions and respond to your comments.

The demonstrator needs to concentrate on words, audience *and* the kit. Talk about multi-tasking! If you know the demonstration so well that you can almost fly on autopilot you will then give yourself the chance to look and listen for signs from the audience. Look for the following:

■ the audience suddenly sits up (interested);
■ the audience leans back (comfortable and reassured);
■ the audience gasps and draws breath (interested);
■ people whisper to their neighbours (interested).

Make a note of what caused the reaction and talk about it after the presentation is over.

A two-handed presentation/demonstration is a good idea for technical demonstrations. If the kit breaks down you may need help. This is horrible when it happens, but Sod's Law tells us it might. Have a series of 'cover-up' phrases ready that you can call on when you need them.

Exercise

Prepare a set of 'cover-up phrases' in case the following happens:
- The kit crashes but can soon be made to work again.
- The kit runs really slowly.
- The sound fails.
- The kit fails to start.

Of course, it goes without saying that you know exactly where you can get help, and you've plotted with the sponsor what you will do if the worst should happen!

It may be hard to see the audience's reaction. You may be a disembodied head, talking in the dark. Perhaps you could come out to the front during the breaks between each part of the demonstration?

The demo may be so loud that your voice will sound weak in comparison. Pitch your voice up and use more volume when the time comes for you to speak. Don't immediately talk about important things the moment the demo stops, use some stock phrases like: 'I'll give you a few moments to digest what you've just seen,' or 'Before we take questions, would anyone like to take a break?' This will give the audience a chance to focus on you and your voice and take their attention away from the screen.

Most demos need to have the lights lowered. The human eye takes longer to adapt to the dark than to brightness (though each takes a few seconds). Always pause for at least five seconds (one-Mississippi, two-Mississippi, three-Mississippi, four-Mississippi, five-Mississippi) before you start rolling the demo. At the end, bring the lights up slowly before you make your way to the front (this gives them a chance to react to the light).

Sometimes you don't know who is in the audience until it's too late. If you have any doubts about who is in the audience and what they are there for, take the time when you are welcoming them to find out. Creating a rapport with an audience before you start is essential to a good demonstration. Once you know what they want you can introduce each demo with the 'This one's for you, Jack' trailer that will make them listen and look actively.

A demonstration is always tuned finely to audience needs. Talking to the sponsor should clear this up. It's very effective to use the names of the people in the audience and to refer to what they do as often as possible (rapport!).

A demonstrator may be comfortable with the kit and the demo but a little unsure about the business issues. The sponsor should have briefed you before, but if there are times when you cannot achieve this, get the audience to tell you about their business. If it's a selling demo, the salesman should always be there anyway.

Exercise

Make a list of the questions you need to ask the sponsor before the demonstration.

Incorporating a demonstration in a presentation

Of course, when most people come to a demonstration they are there because they want to be there and are looking forward to seeing something amazing! This is a lovely situation for the demonstrator/presenter to be in – you are not only showing your audience something that you yourself are enthusiastic about, but they are enthusiastic too. But you still need to think about what they are really there for:

■ to be educated about a new product;
■ to understand the technical side;
■ to be amazed;
■ to be amused;
■ to be impressed;
■ to buy;
■ to compare;
■ to share;
■ to convince;
■ to illustrate;
■ to try;
■ to discuss.

All these are valid reasons, but perhaps some of them require a little more than just a simple demonstration. For instance, 1, 2 and 4 need a 'full bells and whistles' type demo whereas 5,6, and 8 need more of a sales job. 3, 7 and 9 would need background information and 10, 11 and 12 might need some hands-on on the part of the audience – certainly more of a dialogue than a formal demo.

It is always worth asking the 'sponsor' (the person who has requested the session) exactly what it is he/she is trying to achieve and then to tailor the presentation/demo to those needs. Once you know exactly what the audience is looking for, then you can present the whole demonstration in a way that fulfils their expectations. It may well be the same demonstration in most cases, but it is the Introduction to the demo that will set the scene and make it more valuable. This Introduction is the presentation part of the session, as is the ending, where you pull everything together in the light of what the audience wanted to see and why they wanted to see it.

Table 17.2 Demonstration briefing

What the salesperson should tell the demonstrator about the audience:	Full names and job titles
Past history of trading with this company	Where they are from
Company	Location
Home	Special interests
Job-related	Company-related
Personal	Experience:
Technical	Business
Function in the sales process	Decision maker
Adviser	User
Interested party	Finance
Training	Technician
Other	Purpose of visit
Expectations	Timetable (arrival and leaving times)
Salesperson's purpose for visit	Salesperson's expected outcomes

The sales cycle

It is very useful to know where the customer is in terms of the sales cycle. There are lots of sales models to choose from, but they can all be condensed into the stages shown in Table 17.3.

The customer has different needs at each of these stages.

Table 17.3 The sales cycle

AWARENESS	⇨	INTEREST	⇨	DESIRE	⇨	ACTION

Awareness

Here, the customer doesn't really know exactly what they want. They need to be made aware of what is available.

What might a demonstration contain at this point? What would the purpose of the demonstration be?

Interest

The customer is becoming interested in what is on offer, and would like to investigate further.

What might a demonstration contain at this point? What would the purpose of the demonstration be?

Desire

Here the customer is beginning to want to buy, but probably has a great many questions that need answering.

What might a demonstration contain at this point? What would the purpose of the demonstration be?

Action

The sale is nearly in the bag, the customer just needs helping towards the decision. Here objections and worries will surface.

What might a demonstration contain at this point? What would the purpose of the demonstration be?

Opening a demonstration session

Chocks away chaps!! Now is the time to dim the lights, bring up the music and start the demo – but before you do, you need to focus their minds and eyes on what they are about to experience. You will need to cover at least these things:

- What you are going to show them?
- Why you are going to show it?
- How does what you are showing them relate to their business needs?
- How long will it take?
- What should the audience look out for in particular?
- Give interesting details of how the demo was created and why.
- What more might you add?

Running the session

As you go through the demonstrations, one hopes that the audience becomes more and more amazed, and readier and readier to buy. However, all the stimulation they are receiving may lead to the danger of 'information overload'. This might cause them to forget some of the more salient points that you want them to remember afterwards. To stop this happening, you might need to take short breaks between the demonstrations. You can use these breaks to reinforce what they have seen and experienced, and to link what they have seen to their workaday life.

You might use a formula like this:

■ Bring the lights up.
■ Summarize the salient points.
■ Ask them how this would relate to their business.
■ Link to the next presentation.
■ Lower the lights.

What else could you do?

Handling problems

This is a quote from Brian Lecomber – an amazingly experienced pilot and author:

> 'An accident involving an aircraft is rarely the result of a single pilot error or 'plane malfunction. Accidents usually happen when a whole series of small errors and malfunctions occur, concatenating into a major incident.'

It's a fair bet that much the same thing happens in the demonstration room. You can do three things to avoid disasters:

■ Feedforward controls (Where you make sure that everything that is going to happen is as controlled as possible).
■ Concurrent controls (Where you have a series of contingency plans that can swing into action should things start to go wrong).
■ Feedback controls (Where you examine what went wrong and take actions to avoid it happening again).

Exercise

What is likely to go wrong in your demonstrations? What can you put in as feedforward, concurrent and feedback controls?

If a disaster either looms or occurs, you need to have a script ready. Like all emergency procedures, these need to be practised regularly and updated where necessary.

If by any dreadful chance your feedforward, concurrent and feedback controls have not averted the disaster, then you will have to talk your way out of it.

Exercise

Make a list of possible disasters and write a 'recovery script' for each of them.

Summary

The demonstrator has a much harder row to hoe than the presenter and therefore needs all the help and information possible. Salespeople should carefully brief demonstrators about what the audience needs to know and what they are expecting. Forewarned is forearmed, so disaster recovery plans need to be carefully made in advance of the demonstration.

18

Controlling the Audience

Throughout this book I've stressed the importance of finding out just what makes your audience tick, and how very important preparation and rehearsal is. If you have done the research and preparation well you should have no problems with audience control. New presenters have the most vivid imaginations when it comes to what might go wrong, and yet in all the years I've been presenting and teaching presentation skills, I've never come across anyone who had to quell an audience riot.

If a member of the audience is being difficult then there may be many reasons that are nothing to do with you, the presenter, at all. They could be bored, they may disagree with what you are saying, they may have a grudge against your company or the sponsor of the presentation, they may have had a confrontation with their colleagues or family and be feeling generally bad tempered.

The major rule in handling hecklers is to keep your head. Do not take the heckling personally, and unless you have a rapier sharp wit, be very careful about engaging a heckler in any sort of argument. The best way to handle them is to diffuse the situation if you can. If the heckler simply will not pipe down, you can appeal to the audience (they will be on your side anyway) and say something like 'I'm sure other members of the audience have questions or points to make'. If the heckler has really taken against you, then firmly say something like this: 'I know that we disagree on this point, so I'll take it up with you after the presentation.' The secret is never to be drawn into an argument and to be as unfailingly polite as you possibly can be.

If the heckler is drunk or disordered you may have to appeal for help to have him or her ejected. After this has happened, you can calm the atmosphere by saying something along the lines of 'I hope that we're all feeling more comfortable now', and carry on.

What is much more likely to happen is that the audience becomes tired or torpid, particularly if the conference room is hot and humid, or the audience is digesting their lunch. This is what presenters call 'the dead hour' when, even though the audience may be genuinely interested in what you are saying, their metabolism is fighting their interest. If they were in a normal situation and not forced to sit still they could get up and walk around and raise their energy levels; however this isn't possible in a presentation. What the presenter can do is to take the dead hour into account and do one of these things:

■ Give in, lower the lights and show a 10-minute video. This is quite long enough for the sleepy ones in the audience to take a sneaky nap and awake refreshed.

■ Pitch your voice up, speak a little faster and with more emphasis, use more vivid language and make the presentation lively and compelling.

■ Ask them to stand up, find someone they don't know, shake hands with them and introduce themselves. (Not suitable for formal theatre style presentation rooms.) This is really energizing and you will feel the buzz in the presentation room when it happens.

■ Get the audience involved in an activity that will energize them. Prepare a large flip chart sheet with the following questions on it, and ask the audience to pair up with the people on each side and see how many questions they can answer in five minutes.

Flip chart questions for energizing an audience

■ One month has 28 days, of the remaining 11, how many have 30 days?

■ A woman gave a beggar 10 pence. The woman is the beggar's sister but the beggar is not the woman's brother. What is their relationship?

■ Why can't a consultant living near London be buried West of Oxford?

■ Do they have a Fourth of July in England?

■ How can you throw a tennis ball with all your might and have it stop and come right back to you without it hitting a net, a wall or any other obstruction?

■ Two fathers and two sons shot three deer. Each took home one deer. How was that possible?

■ Visualize four horizontal lines, one above the other, now visualize four vertical lines, each one cutting through the horizontal lines. How many squares did you form (do not use paper and pencil)?

■ Six men drove over 150 miles in a car. The trip took two hours, yet no one in the car noticed that they had a flat tyre the whole time. How was this possible?

■ You are sitting in a room with 12 friends. Can any of them sit in a particular place in the room where it would be impossible for you to sit?

■ Seven cars were lined up in a dealer's showroom bumper to bumper. How many bumpers were actually touching each other?

(Answers on p 219.)

Handling interruptions

Many presenters are alarmed at the thought that they might be interrupted by members of the audience; they fear that they might lose their thread or that the presentation may veer off course. Let's think about this for a moment. If the audience is interested enough, confused enough or knows something different, then isn't it a good thing for them to interrupt? In fact, might not the interruption add value to the presentation? If you give the presentation with this in mind, then you will see the interruption as another way of driving your point or a piece of information home.

With some audiences (colleagues, experts, your bosses) you can almost guarantee that there will be interruptions, so legislate for it. You can preface your presentation with something like this: 'We have 20 minutes to cover the subject, and there will be time for questions afterwards. I welcome audience participation, but if I feel that we are getting off the subject I reserve the right to ask you to keep your comments for later.' This serves the double purpose of priming the audience to participate but also keeps them on track.

Summary

Don't be alarmist about audiences – in the main they are polite, interested and good humoured. It is very rare for people to be really nasty when they are part of an audience since they know that the rest of the audience will take the presenter's side. The rules of polite society are usually enough to keep the psychopaths at bay. If you are heckled viciously or members of the audience do behave badly, take control instantly, don't get dragged into a quarrel and don't take it personally.

19

Handling the Media

Sooner or later, you or your company will come into contact with the media. This may be because you need them or because they need you. What is 'the media'?

The media is enormous, the media is influential, the media has the biggest audience you will ever address. The *written* media is huge. At the time of writing there are more than 30 national newspapers, more than 70 regional newspapers and another 20 in Scotland, Ireland and Wales. That is without counting weekly, monthly and quarterly magazines and the trade and free press.

The *broadcasting* media is equally huge – international and national television, national regional and local radio and the growing use of the World Wide Web. 'Media' also includes exhibitions, seminars and trade fairs. The media has a vast, powerful and greedy audience, ever avid for information. This can be an enormous advantage or a minefield depending on which way you look at it.

The secret of successful media management is in the preparation you and your company put in place. Whatever the size of your company or workforce, it is very useful indeed to think (in advance) about how interviews will be handled. Usually it falls to the marketing or public relations department to formulate a plan of action. They need to have a system that will smoothly swing into action whenever an interview with the media is going to happen. It is a complete recipe for disaster if no one knows who should speak to the media, what the message is, who in the media you will be speaking to and what the outcome should be, let alone setting an untrained and unprepared speaker loose on the public.

A competent marketing or PR department will be able to provide (at the very least), the following things:

■ press packs containing up-to-date information about your company, or a website that carries this information;

■ up-to-date information about the media and the personalities involved;

■ the company line on any newsworthy item;

■ an idea of the future direction of the company and its products and services;

■ industry background and competitive information;

■ biographies of key players in the company, and yourself if this isn't prepared;

So, imagine that the marketing department has asked you to do an interview. What do you need to know to feel comfortable about this? The first, and probably most important question is: why are you, in particular, talking to the media anyway? What is your role?

Here are some of the interview roles that you might have to fulfil:

■ Spokesperson: that is, the figurehead for the company in this particular interview who will authoritatively put across the company line.

■ Expert: that is, someone whose professional knowledge will allow them to speak authoritatively on the subject in hand.

■ Trouble shooter: that is, the person in the company who is in charge of damage control if your company has been involved in a news story in a negative way.

■ Involved party: that is, the person from the company who has knowledge of exactly what has happened and can add detail to the main story.

■ Panelist: that is, someone who can add the company's point of view to the general topic being discussed.

The second question is: what does the media want from you, what are they looking for? Here are some of the possibilities:

■ A quote, that is, a sound bite (usually about two minutes' worth) that will add to the main news story.

■ Input from an expert, where the subject matter is complex and the interviewer needs someone who can explain it cogently.

■ An explanation of why an event has happened, both positive and negative aspects.

■ A political statement of the company's attitude to the news item.

■ A victim – someone who can be blamed for any misdeed.

■ An advertisement (this often comes from the trade press) where you can compare your company's offerings to others or present your company to the market.

The third question is to do with which type of media will be interviewing you. These are the main media outlets:

- Local radio, where (unless there has been a terrible disaster) they are usually looking for a local interest story and are generally benign.
- Local newspapers, who are also generally benign, and unless you are being asked for information for a full article, are usually looking for a short(ish) quote.
- Trade press who usually give you a chance to talk about how wonderful your company, product, service offering, cutting edge technology is and will continue to be. These interviews are almost always done well before the publication date.
- National magazines, again, usually done well before publication date, who allow you to expound at length about your company.
- National radio. Here, unless you are in the news or into disaster recovery mode where there may well be pressure on you to give an immediate interview, the interview will probably be pre-recorded.
- National press, as above, with same-day (evening papers) or next-day publication, you may be pressured into immediate response.
- Local television, where, unless it is a pre-planned feature, you may not have as much time to prepare as you would like.
- National television: again, if it is a news item, they like an immediate response.

The fourth question concerns what they want to talk about:

- You, because you are particularly newsworthy (awards, knighthoods and so on) or notorious.
- Your company, and how it impacts on the news item.
- You or your actions, particularly if there has been a negative news item.
- Your job or your expertise and wider knowledge on a newsworthy subject, not necessarily solely about your company.

Now you need to know what limits you can put on what you say:

- What you are prepared to talk about. Here you need to know the particular points they want to cover, for example, they are hardly likely to want to know how your invoicing system works if the subject in hand is your new massive expansion or redundancy programme.
- What you are not prepared to talk about and if there are any legal aspects involved. The standard caveats on taboo subjects are often to do

with company confidential information where knowledge about new products, pricing or innovations may give your competitors an advantage. If legal disputes are under way or possible in the future it will be almost certain that any information directly relating to these should not be discussed.

■ The company line on the subject. Marketing should certainly know this – if by any awful possibility they don't, go and ask the people in charge before you even consider discussing this.

■ Can you deflect questions if necessary – you are not generally expected to be the ultimate expert on everything? Or if you don't know the answer, go and find someone who does.

Where will the interview take place?

■ In your office – this is probably the most favourable place for an interview. We are always more at ease on our own patch. It also means that you have support at hand. However it is useful, not to say sensible, to make sure that the surroundings are as flattering as possible to you and your company, and also that the background noise and bustle is suitable. A shop floor, while fascinating would be too noisy for a successful interview.

■ Over the phone. Again, provided that the background noise is minimal and that you have all the information you need in front of you, not an altogether alarming prospect, but if you need time to prepare you can always ask them to ring back.

■ At their offices. Not as easy – you are away from your comfort zone, but as long as you have all the relevant information either with you or in your head, this should not be too daunting.

■ Neutral ground. Again, not too daunting unless you cannot control what is going on in the background (the interviewer should do this anyway).

■ In a studio. Unless you are familiar with recording studios this can be alarming. Take time to get to know your surroundings and talk to the sound engineers, producer and interviewer about what to expect.

■ On the doorstep. 'Door-stepping' is when a journalist thrusts a notebook, microphone or camera into your face without warning, and is only permissible in the cases of mass murderers who have got away with it, starlets who want the exposure and politicians who love giving interviews anyway. There are, in fact, very few times when you might be asked to give an off the cuff interview (for example outside a court house after a particularly lively case, or at the scene of an accident or event.) A dignified but non-verbal exit left is probably the best strategy.

Who will be interviewing you?

■ A local reporter or journalist, probably looking for a local interest story or a comment on a local issue.

■ A national media interviewer, looking for information about a national and far-reaching story.

■ A national figure (noted for being nasty to interviewees) who may well have a sub-agenda. For instance, asking for an interview on your views on immigration policy, which you do want to talk about, then switching to the latest misdemeanor of a cabinet colleague, which you don't.

■ An interested party, who wants to know the facts.

■ A sympathetic ear, who wants to hear your side of the story.

■ A vested interest, who only wants to hear things that add to their side of the story.

■ A single-issue fanatic, who will certainly only want to present their side of the story.

Knowing the answers to all these questions is the first stage of preparation.

Just before an interview – taking control

There is no law written in stone that says that you have to give an immediate interview over the phone or in person. In fact, you should never do this. No deadline is so tight that the interviewer cannot wait for 30 minutes until you get back to them.

The secret to giving a successful interview (from your point of view, that is) is to take control as early as possible. If the approach is by phone (and it usually is) then ask for their name, number and what they want to talk about and tell them that you'll get back to them if you decide to give the interview. Then get in touch with your media department.

Exercise

The phone rings. It's your local newspaper or radio station. They want to know your feelings about a report that says that your company is responsible for a faulty product that has put children's lives at risk. This is untrue, but unless a really credible answer is forthcoming, the public will be given a wrong impression about your company and your products. What should you say to the reporter asking for the interview?

Preparing for an interview – the five-step preparation process

If you are going to give the interview then you need to prepare yourself first. Slow down and breathe deeply. You are in control. Now follow this five-step process to get your thoughts clear.

Step 1

Decide what you want to say. Limit this to no more than three or four points. The public won't remember more than this and you don't need to cloud your message with too many points. What is your main point? This is the memory that the listener or reader will take away from the interview.

Step 2

Find evidence to back up your main point, evidence that will persuade the listener or reader to believe you.

Step 3

Practise your main points by saying them aloud in at least three different ways and make notes. You may not need these notes at the interview, but writing them down will make them stick in your memory.

Step 4

What are your limits? What subjects are out of bounds and why? Think about what you are actually going to say if faced with off-limit questions.

Step 5

Decide what you will say at the end of the interview and practise it.

Getting help before an interview

You are not alone! There should be a professional group in your company that has experience in handling the media. If you have any worries – go to them first. (I'd always recommend talking to the experts before being interviewed anyway!) If you're really out on your own, call a friend who knows about the information the interviewer is looking for and discuss what worries you and what you need to talk about.

It is particularly important to get in touch with the professionals if you feel that the interview is in any way threatening. Of late there has been a vogue for so called 'penetrating interviewing techniques' where the interviewer talks over the interviewee and cuts the interviewee off aggressively. To handle this sort of interview well takes years of skill and a skin like an elephant. This style of interviewing, however, is by no means the norm: in fact, most journalists and media people are as polite and kind as we are ourselves. They need a truthful and accurate story and will work towards that.

If there are any techniques in being interviewed, they are the following.

Do not lie – ever!

A politician once said that a lie is just another viewpoint on a subject. Well it's not! Lying is counterproductive. That's why prisons are full of criminals. Aggressive interviewers love people who lie and bend the truth – they just can't wait to prove that the information given is false and that the liar can't be trusted.

All that said, there's no need to include damaging information if you are not asked directly about it – equally there's no point in pretending that you are only going to be asked about a new pumping station when the main news of the day was the poisoning of half of Wales with water provided by your company.

If you are confronted with the problem of an event where your company or division was really at fault then first, acknowledge that there is a problem and that you and your company regret the trouble the people concerned have undergone. If necessary, explain why the problem has happened and tell the interviewer what you and your company are going to do to put it right. This is the nub of the interview, a positive outcome is what everyone is trying to achieve. There is no need to drag the body about, no matter how much the interviewer may try. What is most important is to clearly communicate what your company is doing and will do in the future to solve the problem and make sure that it won't happen again. Failing to acknowledge that people have been seriously affected by what your company has done will alienate your audience. This does not mean accepting liability (this is why you need to talk to your media group or legal department first) – it simply means that you are showing compassion for the people affected.

Take the example of the 2007 floods. There wasn't very much that could be done about the unusual levels of rain and although heavy rain was forecast, nothing as devastating as this was expected and had not happened for many, many years. To be sure there were a great many precipitating factors, but every night on the television and radio and every day in the newspapers most of the people interviewed (who were not victims of the floods) got the blame. Farmers for taking down hedges, builders for building on flood plains, local government for neglecting upkeep on flood drains or failing to bring in flood barriers on time, the government for not having an effective emergency plan, the fire brigade for being unable to get through the rising waters, the police for not patrolling for looters … it went on and on. Naturally the public and media were looking for someone to blame. The interviewees who came out of this best were the ones who, after sympathizing with the flood victims, freely admitted that there had been lessons to learn and then went on to clearly outline what they were doing to mitigate people's misery, and what their plans were for the future. It is very difficult for people not to become defensive when being interviewed about something that they may or may not have caused to happen. The secret is iron control and remembering that in these cases, concern for the public is a better approach than 'It wasn't me, Guv'.

If you don't know the answer, say so

You may be an expert on the internal pressure of water pumps and the intimate details of chlorine molecules, but you cannot be expected to be an expert on everything from the movement of shares to the political futures of privatized companies. If you are asked a question that is outside your expertise, admit that this is so and tell them that you know a man who can tell them what they need to know.

Stick to your point

Don't be sidetracked into sub-issues. If the interviewer tries to do this, return to your main point. Since most interviews are only a couple of sound bites anyway, most interviewers can't afford the time to wander off the subject.

Don't be drawn into an argument

An interview is not a discussion – it is a search for information. The 'oh, yes it is, oh, no it isn't' type of argument makes both the interviewer and the interviewee look foolish. However – outright misinformation must be corrected, as soon as possible and with dignity.

Be unfailingly polite

Nothing defuses a tense situation as much as politeness. Even though you may want to say it through gritted teeth, say thank you at the end of the interview. I remember seeing an MP rip off his lapel microphone and storm out of the broadcasting studio where he had been faced by a highly aggressive interviewer. To me (and having discussed it with others) he was thereafter known as 'that man who couldn't keep his temper'. The interviewer was known as 'that man who put the wind up xxxx'.

Exercise

Your company has made a serious mistake. You sub-contracted the upkeep of a large sector of your railway network to a company that has since gone bankrupt and cannot be held to account. It has since been discovered that the work done was not only substandard but actually posed a threat to the travelling public. The general consensus is that it was not a case of if, but when, an accident would happen. One sector of line must now be closed for at least three weeks while it is brought up to safety standards. This will lead to great inconvenience to rail users. You have alternative plans for the passengers in place but the press and television are clamouring for blood. Prepare an outline of what you would say at an interview.

Exercise

You have been asked to give a three-minute interview to a local newspaper. You are the Managing Director of a large garden centre, and are very proud of the help you are giving to local schools. (You are helping to run a 'Children's Allotment Scheme' that is proving very popular.) This is a wonderful chance to publicize your garden centre. Prepare an outline of what you are going to say.

The actual interview

There are several things to remember

Look friendly, organized, professional and honest. Look the interviewer in the eye, keep your hands showing, don't touch your face, stand or sit straight, breathe slowly and evenly and keep your voice confident.

Work with the interviewer. Listen to the questions carefully, looking the interviewer in the eyes, and answer crisply. To do this successfully, listen to the question all the way through without starting to formulate the answer in your head, then you have these options:

■ You can deal with it. Answer the question clearly and don't get sidetracked. Give a concrete example to illustrate your point if you can.

■ You can defuse it. Show that you understand the questioner's/audience's concerns. Then answer the question as briefly as you can.

■ You can deflect it. Tell the interviewer that you will hand the question over to someone more qualified to answer or to the person whose real problem it is.

■ You can defer it. Point out that you don't have the required information to answer the question and state only what you know now.

■ You can dismiss it. Either refuse to answer it (outside my remit, confidential information, etc) or point out that this is a biased question and the questioner shouldn't expect an answer.

If you feel that the interview is going off the point, restate your main point firmly, refusing to be deflected.

Exercise

You are being interviewed by a tough but fair interviewer for an article in the trade press. You have been asked what your company is going to do to catch up with the new innovations that your biggest competitor has just announced. You are aware that their announcement is a month ahead of your new launch, but also aware that your new product will not only catch up with theirs, but substantially out-perform it. The problem is that you really don't want to spoil your product launch by letting slip any details at this point.

How could you answer the question?

Handling discussions

You may well be asked to be part of a panel of experts or interested parties. These will almost certainly be a mix of some or all the following:

■ Experts who really know what they are talking about. These are not usually a problem unless you try to pretend an expertise you don't have.

■ Experts who are well outside their field of expertise. These can be a problem if they give out information that contradicts yours – correct them as briefly as possible, without aggression and without using phrases like: 'Don't be ridiculous', 'That's an idiotic thing to say', etc. Correct the information not the person. No one likes a smart alec.

■ People who just want to outshine you and the rest of the panel, whatever their field of expertise. These usually hang themselves, just be patient and wait for the chairperson to intervene.

■ Interested parties who genuinely want to hear your side of things. Lovely!

■ Interested parties who only want to talk about what they know or what they are 'selling'. When it's your turn to speak, try to make comments that show that you have considered all points of view.

■ Vested interests who only want to talk or hear things that add to their side of the story. See above.

■ Single-issue fanatics who only want to put across their side of the story. Stick to your guns.

■ The quiet ones – try to include them in your answer, even appeal directly to them: 'What do you think, Mr Jones?'

When sitting on a panel there is more to control, but at least you should have the help of the chairperson. Keep in mind that it is in the chairperson's interest to keep the members of the panel under control. Concentrate on the following:

■ Getting your point across: respond only to the question in hand, and ignore anyone else's contribution unless it contributes to your point.

■ Stopping interruptions: never look at the interrupter: this only encourages them. Look away from them at the chairperson, look back briefly and ask the interrupter firmly to allow you to finish and look again at the chairperson. You could try a blocking gesture like a hand raised with the palm outwards, facing the person interrupting. This sometimes works. Serial interrupters are difficult to stop. That is the chairperson's duty.

■ Staying out of arguments: keep your sense of proportion and humour. This is not the only time you will ever have to get your point across. A discussion is not a jousting match, it should be a fair exchange of views and the audience is almost always on the side of the courteous and the reasonable.

■ Correcting misinformation: unless it is really trivial you must always correct anything that is untrue if it affects your argument. Do this without becoming shrill.

■ Signing off: thank the chairperson and the audience. Beware of trying to slip in the last word: it doesn't leave the best impression.

Other hints and tips

Appearing on television panel shows and televised interviews

I used to work with someone who regularly appeared on a well-known late-night panel show – she usually asked me to accompany her. Every single time this happened, she was whisked off to makeup and, the first two times, reappeared with a different hairstyle and different makeup. This disconcerted us both. Now where it is understandable that a tidy-up and a shine removal exercise would be good, it is probably not the best thing to have to cope with a new image as well as an audience. Be firm: you should look more like yourself on television – not less.

Quotes database

Start collecting now. Every time you hear or read a quotable quote that you could use in an interview, a method of keeping your end up in a discussion, a graceful way of showing that you care about the public, an effective gambit to deflect a difficult subject, an effective metaphor, simile or example that you could use yourself – write it down (we always tell ourselves that we will remember it but we usually don't).

Debrief after the publication or airing of what you have said. Talk to people who have watched or heard you, ask the marketing or PR department whether what you said fitted in with the company line. Just as you would debrief after a presentation, you need to do the same after a session with the media. (And I don't mean a 'darling, you were wonderful', debriefing either.)

Summary

Love it or loathe it, the media is one of the most effective ways of getting your message across. There is an enormous audience out there that actually wants to hear about what your company, products, services and specialities are all about. With the same attention to planning, setting objectives and preparation that you would give to a presentation, you can keep that enormous audience interested.

20

Training People to Give Presentations

Think back to the very first time you gave a presentation to a live audience. It was probably one of the scariest things you had ever done. It is equally probable that you had had no training at all to prepare you for this. If you are an experienced presenter think back to your last presentation – what have you learned over the years that makes it possible for you to present in a businesslike fashion? This chapter looks at ways of training yourself and others in presentation skills.

Training yourself

A few weeks' effort can make an enormous difference. The following modules are short and effective. If you do a couple a day, you will notice the difference fairly quickly. Also, since you are on your own there is no audience to make you nervous.

First you are going to take a hard look at how you appear to others. We have no idea what we really look like until we have actually seen ourselves performing. The very first thing you need to do is get your hands on a video or digital camera, tape, tripod, playback method and enough space to film in, preferably without a distracting background. Set up the camera and tripod so that you can see yourself from head to foot. Set the video going and walk into camera shot. Stop, turn to face the camera and say to it, 'Hello camera, hello audience, hello everyone. I'm (your name).' Do this several times until you feel you are acting naturally. Now set up the playback. Arm yourself with the following questionnaire.

The entrance

▪ How fast/slowly am I moving? How can I improve this?

▪ How straight/slouched am I? How can I improve this?

▪ How quickly did I start? How can I improve this?

▪ Did I look straight into the camera? How can I improve this?

▪ Did I smile? How did I look? How can I improve this?

▪ Did I make any gestures? How can I improve this?

▪ How did I hold my hands? How can I improve this?

▪ What did my voice sound like? How can I improve this?

After the playback, study the notes you have made and do the same thing all over again, working really hard to make the changes you feel that you need. This will probably feel artificial and peculiar, but the more you do it the more you will take control of what you are doing. Bearing in mind that you are the only person who can do this, this is the first step on the journey to polishing your presentation skills. Review your performance and repeat the exercise until you have found the style that you feel most comfortable with and which looks and sounds the best to you.

Now you need to work on the speed, articulation and projection of your voice. Look at this verse:

I sit in solemn silence in a dull, dark dock
In a pestilential prison with a life long lock,
Awaiting the sensation of a short sharp shock
From a cheap and chippy chopper on a BIG BLACK BLOCK.

You will notice that it contains many plosives (the consonants that make our voice crisp and authoritative). Read it aloud a few times and then set up the camera again and film yourself reciting it. First try it softly, then loudly, then stressing the plosives:

I SiT in solemn silence in a Dull DarK DoCK
In a PesTilential Prison with a life long loCK,
AwaiTing the sensation of a shorT sharP shoCK
From a cheaP and chiPPy choPPer On a BiG BlaCK BloCK

Listen to the recording and fill in the following questionnaire:

▪ How loudly/softly was I speaking, and how should I change this?

▪ How slowly/quickly was I speaking, and how should I change this?

▪ Is my articulation crisp enough and how should I change this?

▪ Was my speed altered when I deliberately articulated the plosives?

You will probably notice that when you made an enormous effort to stress the plosives it sounded really peculiar inside your head, but didn't sound particularly odd when you heard it back. This is because what you hear inside your head while you are speaking is not the same thing that the audience hears. Not only are the acoustics different, but your voice resonates differently. You will also notice that it takes a considerable amount of effort to alter your voice. You will need to repeat this exercise until you can speak as clearly as you need to.

Now move on to modulation, pause and gesture. Set up the camera and record yourself saying the following phrases:

■ We have absolutely no idea why this has happened.

■ There are so many factors that have to be taken into account.

■ The spread of this virus, unless we can stop it, will close down the entire network within an hour.

■ There are many, many ways that each and every one of us can make this work.

■ Why is it taking so long for the public to realize that we are serious about this?

■ Who on earth can tell what will happen in the future?

■ This is the only way we can make this project work. Until these standards are set, we have no chance of success.

Make a real effort to use your voice flexibly, varying pitch and tone, using stress and pause and volume. Think about where you could use a gesture to emphasize your point.

First, watch the recording back without the sound and then cover the screen and listen to your voice only. Then fill in the following questionnaire:

■ Did I use pause effectively, could I have done more?

■ Did my voice modulate as much as I thought? How can I improve this?

■ Was the volume okay? Did my voice drop at the end of the phrases? Can I improve this?

■ Were my gestures effective? Can I improve them?

■ Was my stance authoritative? Can I improve this?

Re-record the phrases, making them almost ridiculous in their intensity until your voice becomes more flexible and interesting. Remember, you are trying to extend the range of your voice and to do this you need to be 'over the top' before you feel comfortable with it.

Now you need to work with your script. Firstly, look all the way through it and condense your message to less than 100 words. Record this and watch it back. Fill in the following questionnaire:

■ Was my message clear? How can I improve it?
■ Are the points I'm making in the right order – both logically and for impact?
■ Is the language I'm using positive and dynamic?
■ Do I look as if I believe what I'm saying?
■ When the time comes for the whole presentation, do I have enough examples and illustrations?
■ What will the audience like and dislike? What should I do about this?
■ What questions will this presentation raise in the audience's minds? How will I answer them?

Record the whole thing again, making any changes as necessary. Doing this several times helps you to learn your presentation and polish up your delivery.

Training others

When you work in a team, you could all get together and run group training courses. These are particularly successful if you allow each person in the group to run a module – training people is a presentation in itself and so will polish up the group members as they take turns to be 'teacher'. The other great benefit of group training is that you have an audience who knows what you are trying to achieve, and will give hard and truthful feedback.

Using the chapters in this book as a basis, here are some modules you might use for group training.

Presentation skills modules

Module: 'Introducing yourself'

(Takes five minutes, maximum.) This is videoed, watched back and critiqued and then used as a basis for planning what changes each person wants to make to their presentation style. Individual 'hit lists' are drawn up and critique cards collected up and distributed.

Module: Why make a presentation at all?

This can take the form of a group discussion on what presentations are trying to do. Discuss these options: giving instructions, passing on information, persuading people to change their minds, persuading people to accept a course of action, identifying problems that might exist or looking for potential problems, presenting strategic recommendations, selling a product, service or idea, recommending decision alternatives, teaching skills, communicating bad/good news, reporting progress. Get the group to come up with recipes for doing these things.

Module: Making a splendid first impression

Get the group to draw up a recipe for instant and lasting charisma, plus how to handle opening nerves and the trembles using a videoed exercise to practise these factors.

Module: How communication happens

Discuss exactly what happens when people communicate and what can go wrong.

Module: How people listen

Consider how personality influences listening, how to cause active listening – use the listening exercise in Chapter 4.

Module: Remembering and forgetting

Consider how to make your message memorable. Do a group exercise illustrating how people process new information, which should result in a checklist 'how to make your message stick'.

Module: Your voice

Posture, pause, projection, pronunciation, pace, precision, presence, presentation and above all – *breathing*.

The authoritative voice. An interactive session with individual and group work

Module: Starting a presentation

Effective openings, the call for active listening, setting expectations, catching attention.

Module: *Structuring a presentation*

The use of structure in a presentation, using logical arguments, anecdotes, examples and references. Structuring and prioritizing your arguments.

Module: *Illustrating what you are saying*

This is a group discussion and exercise. What makes visual aids effective, why use handouts? Covers back-up material (reports, breakdowns, etc) and using PowerPoint™ effectively.

Module: *Analysing your audience*

Tailoring your presentation to specific audiences, speaking directly to audience needs.

Module: *Presenting to specialist audiences*

The difference between technical/practical presentations and business presentations.

Module: *Stagecraft*

The role of the Master/Mistress of Ceremonies, presenting to large audiences, staging and directing large/multiple presentations.

Module: *Climax*

Finishing with a bang and not a whimper, the call to action, how to make sure your message is clear, plenary session with group and individual exercises.

Module: *Handling questions and interaction*

Keeping control of the audience, encouraging feedback, backing up your formal message.

Module: *Looking good, looking businesslike*

How do we present ourselves physically? Group sessions on individual style.

Make all the modules highly interactive, with the 'trainer' making the rest of the group do most of the work!

Structuring a course

When you are structuring a course you should take all the following points into consideration:

- What are the objectives?
- Who will be on the course? Numbers, skills, experience, personalities?
- What learning tasks must be set and completed?
- What equipment do I need?
- What methods should I use?
- Use 30–40 minute modules with breaks every 1–1½ hours.
- The trainees should not be asked to work for longer than six hours per day (excluding breaks).
- The lunch break should be at least 60 minutes long, and in a different room from the course.
- Alternate between passive and active. Passive being the lecture/chalk and talk or presentation and active being where the trainees practise for themselves, discuss, prepare or demonstrate.
- Pick something lively to do after the lunch break.
- State the objectives and set the expectations before each new module.
- Summarize at the end of each module, and collect input from each trainee on what they have learned.
- Summarize at the end of each morning and afternoon session, and write down what each trainee has learned.
- On a longer course, recap each morning.
- Check each evening that all objectives are being met.
- When you give out handouts, explain what they are for and how they will best be used.
- Wherever possible, show the links between the modules.
- Reinforce all 'intellectual' learning with role-play, practice sessions and discussion.
- Set tasks very clearly indeed.
- Allow at least quarter of an hour at the end of the course for the 'debrief' session.

21

The Role of the Master of Ceremonies

Mum, Dad, Big Brother, captain, mediator, entertainer, fixer, policeman, warm-up man, nursemaid and God; the MC wears a great many hats, some of them simultaneously. A good MC can raise the standards of a set of presentations enormously; a bad one can scupper the entire enterprise.

So what is an MC for? Certainly they have a great many duties: introducing presentation sessions, handling logistics, time keeping, introducing speakers, tying the different presentations together, recapping the messages, introducing and controlling the question-and-answer session and winding up the whole performance to name but a few, but over and above all these, the MC is there to keep the audience interested, energized and comfortable.

To do this the MC needs to know a great many things: what the presentations hope to achieve, the audience, the presenters and their presentations, the venue and technology, any politics involved, how to keep a cool head, how to keep control and how to energize an audience. This chapter looks at how to be an effective MC.

The MC's duties before the presentations

Hold a meeting with all the presenters and collect their credibility statements and a synopsis of each presentation. Work out with them how the presentations fit together and the order in which they are going to present. See if you can, as a group, come up with a theme that will link them all together. Also discuss what they know about the audience and any issues that they think will arise. Now you can begin to prepare your script.

Start by making a running plan. This should contain every presentation with its timings, when and for how long the breaks will occur, plus locations of coffee and food. It might look something like this.

Table 21.1 Sample conference agenda

TIME	SPEAKER AND SUBJECT	WHERE
10.30	Arrivals. Coffee	The Sunset Room
11.00–11.15	Mary Profit (MC) Opening, welcome and intro Susan Smith	Main Hall
11.15–11.45 11.45–12. 00	Susan Smith 'New Directions in Banking Questions	Main Hall
12.00–12.05	Link from Sue Smith to intro of Joe Bloggs (MC)	Main Hall
12.05–12.45 12.45–1.00	Joe Bloggs 'Security and Internet Banking' Questions	Main Hall
1.00–2.00	Lunch announcement and lunch break (MC)	The Great Hall
2.00–2.15	Reminder of morning presentations, link to intro of Felicity Ffarnes-Barns (MC)	Main Hall
2.15–3.00 3.00–3.15	Felicity Ffarnes-Barns 'Our Financial Future' Questions	Main Hall
3.15–3.45	Announce coffee break (MC)	The Sunset Room
3.45–3.50	Link from Felicity to intro of Giles Brown (MC)	Main Hall
3.50–4.30 4.30–4.45	Giles Brown 'The Role of the Support Desk' Questions	Main Hall
4.45–5.00	Wind up and farewell (MC)	Main Hall

This is a running plan for a day-long conference with an audience of 20 senior staff from an international bank.

You will see from this that the MC has several scripts to write and four question-and-answer sessions to run: the opening welcome and introduction, the closing summary, thank you and farewell, four introductions with three linking statements and the coffee and lunch break announcements.

The opening welcome and introduction

Welcome everyone in the audience. Mention any special guests (for example, 'Good evening, Your Royal Highness, Prime Minister, Ladies and Gentlemen ...). Briefly introduce yourself – you need to do this even if you think everyone knows who you are. Remind the audience of why they are there and what the event will achieve. Outline the agenda briefly. Cover any logistics briefly (what time the event finishes, when and where lunch or coffee breaks will occur, whether there are any handouts and whether there will be time for questions). Then introduce the first speaker and the subject of the first presentation.

All this is very workmanlike and will put the audience at ease, but the MC needs to do more. It should be possible to involve the audience personally if you have had the chance to meet as many as you can before the presentations start. Find out as much as you can about the following things:

■ their names;
■ the company they work for;
■ what they do;
■ what experience they have had with the subject. Do they have any anecdotes?
■ what they are particularly interested in;
■ what worries them.

This will then allow the MC to personalize the introductions and links. For example:

> Good morning ladies and gentlemen, and a warm welcome to this international banking seminar. We are here to examine the new and potentially very profitable area of internet banking. I am Mary Profit, chairperson of the Bankers' Consortium and author of *Banking on the Future*. Today we have four speakers; Susan Smith from the Think Tank Practicus, who will talk about the latest technology in internet banking, an area I know that Mark and Julie and

the IT department are particularly interested in. Then Detective Inspector Joe Bloggs from the Fraud Squad will take us through some of the security issues that internet banking raises ...

After the general introduction the chairperson introduces the first speaker and his subject in more detail (making sure that the audience are encouraged to listen actively), and then leaves the stage. While the speakers are performing, it is up to the chairman to keep an eye on the time and signal discreetly to the speaker if it is time to stop. As the speaker finishes, the chairman returns to the stage to handle the question-and-answer session. Here the chairman opens up the session. If the questions are slow to arrive, the chairman may have to ask a question to get the ball rolling. Something along the lines of 'One thing I have always wondered about on line banking is ...' or 'Inspector Bloggs, could you tell us more about ...?' When the questions come from the audience, it is up to the chairperson to repeat them so that the whole audience has heard them and then hand over to the presenter for his or her answer.

It is also up to the chairperson to deflect or defer unpleasant questions. Because the chairperson is seen to be impartial and authoritative, it is easier for him or her to do this than the presenter.

The chairperson should make a note of the questions that come up and who asked them, so that if questions are deferred, the answers can be sent to the questioner after the presentations are over.

Duties after the presentations

Sending the audience on their way – the chairperson winds up the entire proceedings, thanking the speakers and the audience, handling any last-minute travel news, and wishing everyone bon voyage.

After the conference is over (as soon as possible), the chairperson should hold a de-briefing session for all the people involved in the conference:

■ the speakers and demonstrators;
■ the conference sponsor;
■ the conference organizers;
■ the technical support staff;
■ the venue staff.

A conference debrief should be used and filed for future reference.

Table 21.2 Chairman's debrief sheet

Area	Item	Grading Bad	Fair	Good	Comments and Cures
Conference generally	Timing	☐	☐	☐	
	Cost	☐	☐	☐	
	Relevance	☐	☐	☐	
	Attendance	☐	☐	☐	
Chairman	Authority and control	☐	☐	☐	
	Friendliness	☐	☐	☐	
	Question handling	☐	☐	☐	
	Intro, Links and Summary	☐	☐	☐	
Speakers	(Make a row for each speaker)	☐	☐	☐	
	Voice	☐	☐	☐	
	Performance	☐	☐	☐	
	Content	☐	☐	☐	
	Questions	☐	☐	☐	
Conference organiser	Pre-conference	☐	☐	☐	
	Delegate registration	☐	☐	☐	
	Troubleshooting	☐	☐	☐	
	Documentation	☐	☐	☐	
	Organization	☐	☐	☐	
Technical support	Kit	☐	☐	☐	
	Reliability	☐	☐	☐	
	Troubleshooting	☐	☐	☐	
Venue	Comfort	☐	☐	☐	
	Cleanliness	☐	☐	☐	
	Food	☐	☐	☐	
	Helpfulness	☐	☐	☐	
	Price	☐	☐	☐	
	Equipment provided	☐	☐	☐	
	Timing	☐	☐	☐	

Summary

The chairperson glues a set of presentations together by looking out for the audience's needs and responses and linking the individual presentations together. The chairperson is also in charge of the smooth running of the conference and the follow up debrief. A strong chairperson can make an everyday conference magnificent.

22

Following Up the Presentation

Oh the relief! The presentations are over, you are satisfied with your performance and you think that the audience was pleased with what they heard and saw. But can you be sure? Now is the time to check it out.

It is always an excellent policy to give out feedback forms at the end of the presentations and ask the audience to fill them in and get them back to you.

Here's an example of a feedback form.

Evaluation Form

We would be grateful if you would take a few minutes to complete this form and hand it in at the end of the conference.

How useful do you think this conference has been?

Not at all   Very

1   2   3   4   5   6

How did you rate the quality of the conference?

Poor   Excellent

1   2   3   4   5   6

Do you feel that the conference will be of use to your company?

No   Yes

1   2   3   4   5   6

Evaluation Form speaker page

Speaker name:

Was motivated and enthusiastic about the topic

1   2   3   4   5

Presented the material in an informative manner

1   2   3   4   5

Any other comments:

Speaker name:

Was motivated and enthusiastic about the topic

1   2   3   4   5

Presented the material in an informative manner

1   2   3   4   5

Any other comments:

Conference

1   2   3   4   5   6

Environment

1   2   3   4   5   6

Administration

1   2   3   4   5   6

Refreshments

1   2   3   4   5   6

Venue

1   2   3   4   5   6

What I found most useful from the conference:

What I found least useful from the conference:

Please give any other comments that you feel would help us to improve conferences in the future.

Once you have analysed these in detail you will have a fair idea of what was good and what needs correcting. Now is the chance to correct any problems that the audience may have. You need to get in touch with as many of the members of the audience as you can, particularly if they have been very pleased with the presentation or not satisfied. The presentation after all, doesn't stand on it's own, it is part of a business objective and if you are to succeed in that objective you need to know what the next steps should be.

To prepare for this, think about what you need to know:

■ Did the audience gain the information they needed?
■ How useful will it be to them?
■ Has the presentation helped the sale?
■ Was there anything they would like to know more about?
■ What would they like to do next?

Make sure that you have completed the question tracking form and have it with you when you get in touch with them.

Speaking to the audience in the days after the presentation will also help to reinforce your message.

Now you need to follow up with the rest of the presentation team. You could use a similar feedback form to the Chairperson's debrief form. The purpose of this debrief is not to blame or grumble about the things that went wrong, but to improve what you did well and correct any faults as well as to congratulate your team on getting the job done.

It is all too easy to let the days go by without debriefing. This is a mistake – you will begin to forget the details within 24 hours, so analyse the feedback and hold the follow up meeting as quickly as possible. Only when this is done can you really give a sigh of relief and relax.

23

Alternatives to Presentations

Bearing in mind all the expense, effort and stress of presentations, there are several other ways of communicating information that can be just as effective. Indeed, in some cases a presentation might be counter-productive. If the information that needs to be communicated is something that seriously affects/involves the group who will be listening to it, then the group's input is vital. A presentation where that group has to sit quietly and listen to something to which they are eager to contribute will only frustrate them. A group discussion, meeting or teleconference or conference call is a much better option.

Equally, when you know that the audience want to ask questions rather than listen to a full presentation, an interview or news conference is more suitable.

This chapter looks at how to make meetings, teleconferences and news conferences time efficient and successful.

Successful meetings

The importance of agendas

Bad meetings waste more time than almost any other business activity. However, a little careful planning can turn a poor meeting into a successful one.

Table 23.1 Effective and ineffective meetings

EFFECTIVE MEETINGS	INEFFECTIVE MEETINGS
Have an agenda	Have no stated purpose
Start on time	Start late
Finish on time	Finish late
Only involve relevant people	Involve Uncle Tom Cobbley and all
Have a chairman	Have no leader
Stick to the agenda	Have no agenda
Provide refreshments	Have no breaks and no refreshments
Happen in comfortable and well prepared rooms	Happen in broom cupboards and noisy offices
Last no longer than 1½ hours	Last for absolutely ages
Have no more than 12 people at them	Have more than 20 people at them
Allow everyone to contribute	Ignore the thoughtful and quiet people
Stick to the subject	Ramble all over the place
Have clear outcomes	Have no outcomes
Are well prepared by all participants	Are never prepared
Are lively	Are soporific
Are not interrupted	Are interrupted
Make decisions where necessary	Never make a decision at all
Are interesting	Are boring
Allow time for networking and socializing	Happen in a vacuum
Never waste time	Waste hours and hours
Are very, very rare indeed	Happen all the time!

Tasks necessary for any meetings

Setting the agenda

Even very short, ad hoc meetings need an agenda and a set of objectives. This list of 'things to do' and what the meeting hopes to achieve focuses the minds of the attendees and keeps the meeting on track.

Here's a proposed agenda and objectives for an editorial meeting.

Table 23.2 Agenda and objectives sheet

EDITORIAL MEETING
Date: *3rd October 2008*   **Time:** *9.30am*
Duration: *2½ hours*
Location: *Conf Room 3*
Logistics: *HP/Screen/Flip chart and pens*

Attendee Name	Attendee Role	Contribution
Bill Jones	Managing Director	Chair meeting
John Jackson	Financial Director	Update on costings/budget
Liz Third	Editorial Director	Update on contractual issues
F Ffarnes-Barnes	PA to Bill Jones	Minutes and logistics
Jack Brown	Chief Editor (Smithson & Co)	Update on deadlines problem
Graham Green	Print Manager (Smithson & Co)	Update paper prices

Agenda

Time	Item	Who
9.30	Welcome, agenda, general update	Bill Jones
10.00	Smithson Update	Graham Green
10.30	Problems with contractual issues	Liz Third
11.00	Proposed solution	Graham Green
11.15	Discussion	All
11.50	Final agreement, action lists, close	All

OBJECTIVES
- *To solve the paper price problems arising from contract QT/12*
- *To find a solution to the late running of this contract*
- *To forward plan for completion of contract by 30/11/2008*

OUTCOMES

ACTIONS

Name	Action	Timescale	Done

Once the agenda has been set then it needs to be distributed to the attendees to get agreement that the agenda covers what is necessary. This also gives the people who are going to speak at the meeting time to prepare what they are going to say.

Now the logistics need to be sorted out. The organizer needs to find out if information needs to be displayed and how will this be done, and if people will need handouts, and if so who will prepare them. For formal meetings someone will need to keep a record of what has been said (minutes). Minutes are a legal account of what has been said at formal meetings and must be passed as a fair account by all who have attended the last meeting at the start of the next meeting. They must also be distributed to all the attendees as quickly as possible after the meeting. The minute taker must be completely impartial, with no interpretation and no omissions; each speaker's name must be noted down, all points must be covered, and all dissension noted. To do this, the minute taker should be assertive and ask people to repeat what they said if they can't be heard. The minute taker should ask for clarification if needed, ask people not to interrupt, ask the chairman for support if necessary. An attendee map of who is sitting where (with the names spelled correctly) is extremely useful.

It goes without saying that meetings should not be interrupted, so message taking and message boards should be organized.

Speaking at a meeting

Since effective meetings should be as short as possible, the speakers at a meeting should be as succinct as possible. Speakers should be encouraged to talk only about the items on the agenda. Anything that the audience already knows should be left out and frequent appeals for input from the rest of the attendees should be sought. The speakers should watch the audience closely, responding to their reactions promptly.

It is the chairperson who runs the meeting. Even a small meeting needs a chairperson.

Chairperson's duties

■ Briefing the speakers by letting them know exactly what they need to contribute to the meeting (remember, only the people who need to be at the meeting should be there – no passengers).

■ Starting the meeting off (exactly on time) with a welcome statement, reminder of objectives and run through the agenda. A good chairperson will quickly involve the audience, encouraging them to contribute right from the start. Because people see the chairperson as an authority, it is important that the chair doesn't contribute to discussions until everyone has had a chance to speak. This is tough for highly involved chairpersons, but it will pay great dividends in terms of allowing people to get all their concerns out into the open, rather than following the chairperson's lead.

■ Chairing the meeting and keeping control. Lively meetings are great, even if hostility is expressed – however, when side discussions develop or personalities intrude into the matters at hand, the chairperson needs to intervene to keep the meeting on track.

■ Introducing the speakers and their subjects. This keeps the speakers to their subjects.

■ Recording the meeting, or making sure that someone is taking the minutes.

■ Handling questions by making sure that everyone has heard the questions and understands them, and if necessary, choosing who will respond to them.

■ Helping decision making by asking for a vote or majority opinion.

■ Updating information if there are any misunderstandings.

■ Summarizing at the end of each speaker's slot, and tying the different agenda items together.

■ Closing the meeting, making the call to action, allocating the follow-up actions, setting the time and venue for the next meeting and ensuring that the minutes are written up and distributed to everyone who was at the meeting within two days at the most.

Attendees' checklist for meetings

■ Are the objectives clear to you?

■ Are the objectives clear to all those attending the meeting?

■ Do you have an agenda?

■ Has this been distributed?

■ Do you have the minutes from the last meeting?

■ What is the purpose of the meeting?
  - Sharing experiences
  - Keeping myself informed
  - Informing others
  - Training
  - Brainstorming new ideas

- Solving problems
- Evaluating proposals
- Making decisions
- Airing grievances
- Obtaining advice
- Giving advice to others
- Motivation
- Providing targets / deadlines
- Consulting interested parties

Which is the most important of these for this meeting?

Leaders' checklist

■ Do we really need to have this meeting?

■ Are there any alternatives to meeting face to face?

■ What are the objectives for this meeting?

■ Who will need to be at the meeting to make sure that we meet the objectives?

■ What is the benefit of meeting these objectives?

■ What will the meeting cost?

■ What logistical support do we need for the meeting?

■ Has the agenda been prepared and distributed?

■ Does everyone know when the meeting will start and finish?

■ Has everyone received all relevant background material?

■ Has each participant prepared their contribution?

■ Does everyone need to be there for the whole of the meeting?

Attendees' personal checklist

■ Do I really need to attend this meeting?

■ Have I read the agenda and objectives for this meeting?

■ Is there any alternative to this meeting?

■ Do I know the timing / location of this meeting?

■ Have I organized my schedule so that I can get to the meeting on time?

■ What do I want to contribute to the meeting?

■ What background material / knowledge do I need for this meeting?

- If I am making a presentation at this meeting, have I prepared? What equipment will I need for my presentation?
- Will I need to follow up after this meeting?

Organizer's checklist

- Is the room for the meeting booked?
- Has every attendee confirmed receipt of the agenda, objectives and location?
- Are there enough chairs / tables for the meeting?
- Do we need to organize parking for this meeting?
- Are refreshments organized?
- What equipment do we need for this meeting?
- Does the equipment work?
- Who is keeping minutes at this meeting?
- Who will receive the minutes from this meeting, and when?
- Do any of the speakers at the meeting have any special needs?

Teleconferencing and video conferencing

The use of teleconferencing allows people to participate in regional, national or worldwide meetings without actually leaving their local office, so saving travelling time and expenses. These conferences can be planned only hours ahead of time instead of days or weeks. The technology is easily used, consisting of either a telephone conference centre (voice only) or video cameras and telephone lines (voice and vision) or linked computers with a video and voice link.

Tele- or video conferences are very focused, chit-chat is kept to a minimum and the chairperson has control over who is speaking.

There are however, one or two disadvantages of tele or video conferencing: there is always the possibility of technical failure, so test the kit thoroughly before starting and have technical help available.

It can be difficult to build close relationships between group members since there is less socializing than in face-to-face meetings.

What to look out for with tele- or video conferencing

Near the start of the conference each person should introduce himself or herself. Don't all talk at once. The chairman must keep firm control and introduce each speaker, each time they speak. There may also be a slight time lag between the voice speaking and the video image, so each person should speak a little more slowly than usual. Follow the rules for using a microphone (Chapter 12) and speak as clearly as you can.

Be aware that with video equipment throughout the room you may be on camera at any time so be circumspect about any comments you may make or any fidgeting and so on.

Video conferencing and interactive computer programs are increasingly being used in schools and educational establishments and can act as a useful alternative to a full-blown presentation or teaching session. They may take as much time to develop as a presentation but they do have the excellent advantage that they can be viewed at a time that completely suits the audience.

Summary

When you think about the sheer expense of staging presentations, it is always worth considering alternatives. Both meetings and teleconferencing are infinitely more cost effective than full-blown presentations, but they will need planning and organizing with just as much care as a presentation.

Handling Disasters

If it can happen, then at some time in your presentation career it probably will:

■ no audience;
■ no presentation room;
■ no accommodation;
■ no electricity;
■ no guest speakers;
■ no food;
■ no equipment;
■ no software;
■ no voice;
■ a plague of greenfly;
■ an earthquake;
■ a flood;
■ the hotel catches fire;
■ no handouts;
■ no light;
■ food poisoning.

Well – delivery vans break down, power supplies fail, nature cannot be controlled, conference administrators can make mistakes, people are only human and if there's a spanner about, it often finds its way into the works!

The first and most important rule is: don't pretend it hasn't happened.
Secondly: define the exact problem.
Thirdly: don't panic, you will gain Brownie points for being calm.
Fourthly: keep a careful record.
Fifthly: let the audience know what is happening.

Sixthly: don't be afraid to cancel the presentation if the circumstances merit it.

Seventhly (and most importantly): natural disasters apart, most break-downs are the result of poor communication on the part of the speaker, the conference organizer, the venue manager or the delivery man and not the audience. So – check, check and check again that everyone knows what is expected of them, and cross-check whenever possible.

Onto specific cures. Obviously if you have no venue, no light and no voice, you will have to cancel the presentation and reschedule, but that apart there are some disasters that can be ameliorated.

No kit for the slides: always ask for a flip chart to be available, and use that. I always have a printout of my slides with me that can be turned into a handout and distributed to the audience if I cannot use the slide show.

No power: this is not your fault, and the audience will understand. While the power is being put back on, organize a question-and-answer session.

No audience: find out why. If they can get there in a reasonable time scale, start the presentation when they arrive, if not, cancel.

No food: go out to the nearest pub. Make sure that they get back on time.

No guest speakers: have a fill-in session prepared. Give the absentee speaker hell when you see them – they are responsible for finding a replace-ment, not you.

No handouts: always have a master copy with you that the venue can use to photocopy for you. If they cannot, send the handouts to the audience either electronically or by post.

Food poisoning: cancel the presentation, call a doctor, sue the hotel!

Natural or man-made disasters: take no chances with anyone's security – audience first, presenter second. Get out. Record what happened (as soon as possible), report back and get the audience home safely. Make sure that loss records are made rapidly and accurately.

Venue problems (mis-booking, external noise, appalling service, food poisoning, etc): keep careful records (signed by other observers). Take it up – as soon as possible – with the manager (not a minion). Refuse to sign the bill. Report to your manager or the presentation's sponsor. Write a careful itemized letter of complaint and take legal advice where necessary.

Summary

Total disasters are rare – take an organized attitude to things that go wrong, and keep a cool head. As long as the audience is kept up-to-date on what is happening, they will be on your side, it's when they are left in the dark that they become restive.

Appendix: Templates, Checklists and Reminders

Master checklist

ITEM	COURSE	DONE
Mobile phone	All	
Phone charger	All	
Laptop	All	
Laptop power cable	All	
Laptop mouse	All	
Laptop mouse (portable)	All	
Mouse connector	All	
Mouse mat	All	
Laptop connector to projector	All	
Connector to projector	All	
Projector	As needed	
Projector power	As needed	
Screen	As needed	
Camera	As needed	
Camera power	As needed	
Camera to projector cables	As needed	
Speakers	As needed	
Speaker power	As needed	
Speaker cables	As needed	
Tripod (small)	As needed	

ITEM	COURSE	DONE
Tripod (large)	As needed	
Video tapes	As needed	
CDs for laptop	As needed	
External disk drive	As needed	
Chocolate box extension	As needed	
Gaffer tape	All	
Digital camera	As needed	
Batteries	As needed	
Digital camera power	As needed	
Master disk	All	
Master documentation	All	
Delegate documentation	All	
Exercise documentation	All	
Feedback forms	All	
Backup reading (my books)	All	
Flip charts	All	
Pens	All	
Extra pads	All	
Blu tac	All	
Stickit pads	All	
Index cards		
Treasury tags		
Hole punch		
Paper for notes		
Red alarm clock	All	
Timer	All	
Diary	All	
Daybook	All	
Laminates/summary sheets	As needed	
Pins	All	

ITEM	COURSE	DONE
Gold stars	All	
Sweeties	All	
Business cards	All	
Name labels/tags	All	
Tent cards	All	

Personal profile

This is about how you like to learn, and how you like to present.			
Set 1. Leisure pursuits	A	B	C
How do you like to spend your leisure time?	*Reading/listening to music/ TV/radio*	*Physical activities*	*Group activities*
Set 2. Learning simple tasks (things like learning to use household equipment, using new tools, etc)			
How did you approach the task?	*Made a plan and read the manual*	*Went ahead with no planning*	*Asked for advice*
What did you use to help yourself?	*Reading matter or reference matter*	*Trial and error*	*Found an expert*
How did you consolidate your learning?	*Scheduled regular practice sessions*	*Improved by doing*	*Asked someone to test it or check what I had done*
How did you refine those skills?	*Set incremental goals*	*Just kept on doing*	*Discussed progress with others*
Set 3. Hobbies and pastimes (like sports, music, model making, collecting)			
How do you find out more about the hobby or pastime?	*Books, reference matter*	*By doing it*	*Clubs, friends*

How often do you spend time on your hobby?	*Regularly*	*Spasmodically*	*When there's a meeting*
Have you taken any courses or qualifications in the hobby or pastime?	*Yes or intend to*	*No*	*Not unless the group wants to*
Set 4. Business skills (MBA, professional qualifications, IT skills, handling new equipment/procedures, etc)			
Why did you learn the new skill?	*Part of a personal plan*	*It just happened*	*Peer pressure or the need to keep up with the group*
How did you learn it?	*By yourself or from reference material*	*By doing it*	*By asking others, having a mentor, discussion*
How did you refine or develop the new skill?	*Practice, reading/research*	*By doing it*	*Help from friends*

Self-assessment

We would like you to fill in the following table. It is a self-assessment of your skills and will help us to tailor the course to your specific needs.

Look at the categories below and give yourself a score.

When I think about the way I make presentations now, I consider that the way I handle the following things is:

STRUCTURE OF THE PRESENTATION	Good	Fair	Poor	Oh dear!
Organization				
Logic				
Interest to the audience				
Presentation of benefits				
Positive start				
Powerful ending				
Good, concrete examples				
Length				
Balance between theory and reality				

VOICE	Good	Fair	Poor	Oh dear!
Clarity				
Modulation				
Pace				
Strength				
Tone				
Articulation				
Personal mannerisms				
Clarity throughout the presentation				

STANCE AND POSTURE	Good	Fair	Poor	Oh dear!
Confidence				
Gestures				
Eye contact with the audience				
Personal appearance				
Use of the presentation area				

VISUAL AIDS	Good	Fair	Poor	Oh dear!
Clarity				
Interest				
Number of slides				
Added value				
Equipment handling				

Feedback sheets

Presentation 1

Presenter's name:_____

Feedbacker's name:_____

Please rate the presenter on the following points. Please be specific about what they did well and what they need to change. If they need to change or practise a particular factor, please give advice on how they could make things better.

	Must change	Needs practice	Very nice	Comments (be specific)
Audibility and articulation				
Stance and gesture				
Eye contact				
Good start				
Good end				
Content				
Contact and involvement with the audience				
Speed				

Presentation 2

Presenter's name:_____

Feedbacker's name:_____

Please rate the presenter on the following points. Please be specific about what they did well and what they need to change. If they need to change or practise a particular factor, please give advice on how they could make things better.

	Must change	Needs practice	Very nice	Comments (be specific)
Audibility and articulation				
Stance and gesture				
Eye contact				
Good start				
Rousing ending				
Content				

Contact and involvement with the audience				
Speed				
Call to action				
Summary (not a repeated agenda!)				
Reminder of self				

Presentation 3

Presenter's name:_____

Feedbacker's name:_____

Please rate the presenter on the following points. Please be specific about what they did well and what they need to change. If they need to change or practise a particular factor, please give advice on how they could make things better.

	Must change	Needs practice	Very nice	Comments (be specific)
Audibility and articulation				
Stance and gesture				
Eye contact				
Good start				
Rousing ending				
Content				
Contact and involvement with the audience				
Speed				
Call to action				
Summary (not a repeated agenda)				

Reminder of self				
A theme of some sort				
Good benefits				
Visuals				

Presentation 4 (the final presentation)

Presenter's name:_____

Feedbacker's name:_____

Please rate the presenter on the following points. Please be specific about what they did well and what they need to change. If they need to change or practise a particular factor, please give advice on how they could make things better.

	Must change	Needs practice	Very nice	Comments (be specific)
Audibility and articulation				
Stance and gesture				
Eye contact				
Good start				
Rousing ending				
Content				
Contact and involvement with the audience				
Speed				
Call to action				
Summary (not a repeated agenda)				
Reminder of self				
A theme of some sort				

Reminder of self				
A theme of some sort				
Good benefits				
Visuals				

Delegate kit

Title page
Conference Title:
Sponsored by:
Location:
Address:
Date:
Duration:
Contact:
Location map and directions page:
Map here

BY ROAD   *BY RAIL*   *BY TAXI*
                       BUSES   *AIRPORTS*
                                       PARKING

Meeting rooms
Dining room and coffee lounge
Hearing aid loops
Programme Page

TIME	EVENT	SPEAKER

There will be time for questions at the end of each presentation. Handouts will be provided.

Delegate List Page

Delegate name	Company

Biography Pages

Presentation pages

(The slides that will be used in the presentations.)

Evaluation form

We would be grateful if you would take a few minutes to complete this form and hand it in at the end of the conference.

How useful do you think this conference has been?

Not at all   Very

1   2   3   4   5   6

How did you rate the quality of the conference?

Poor   Excellent

1   2   3   4   5   6

Do you feel that the conference will be of use to your company?

No   Yes

1   2   3   4   5   6

Speakers

Speaker name:

Was motivated and enthusiastic about the topic

| 1 | 2 | 3 | 4 | 5 |

Presented the material in an informative manner

| 1 | 2 | 3 | 4 | 5 |

Any other comments

Speaker name:

Was motivated and enthusiastic about the topic

| 1 | 2 | 3 | 4 | 5 |

Presented the material in an informative manner

| 1 | 2 | 3 | 4 | 5 |

Any other comments

Conference Environment

Administration

| 1 | 2 | 3 | 4 | 5 | 6 |

Refreshments

| 1 | 2 | 3 | 4 | 5 | 6 |

Venue

| 1 | 2 | 3 | 4 | 5 | 6 |

What I found most useful from the conference:

What I found least useful from the conference:

Please give any other comments that you feel would help us to improve conferences in the future.

Sample course questionnaire

Attendee Name: Presentation Title: Date:

Please indicate your feelings about the presentation by selecting a grading for each question.

| 1=Unacceptable | 2=Fair | 3=Good | 4=Excellent |

		1	2	3	4
1.	How do you rate the venue?	1	2	3	4
2.	How do you rate the organization?	1	2	3	4

3.	How useful was the presentation?	1	2	3	4
4.	How do you rate the presenter?	1	2	3	4
5.	How do you rate the handouts?	1	2	3	4
6.	How did the equipment behave?	1	2	3	4
7.	What was the timing like?	1	2	3	4
8.	Please grade each speaker.				
	– Speaker 1	1	2	3	4
	– Speaker 2	1	2	3	4
9.	Was there anything you would have left out of the presentation?				
10.	Was there anything you would have liked to include?				
11.	Are there any comments you would like to add?				

Rehearsal checklist

Rehearsal Checklist		
Time (start/end)	Subject (what the speaker is talking about)	Comments (what went well, what went badly. How this can be changed)
…	…	…

OVERALL IMPRESSIONS	Good	Fair	Awful
Speed			
Volume			
Modulation			
Gesture			
Use of vocabulary			
Quality of slides			
Organization			
Logic			
Interest to the audience			
Presentation of benefits			
Positive start			
Powerful ending			
Good, concrete examples			
Length			
Balance between theory and reality			
Question handling			

VOICE	Good	Fair	Awful
Clarity			
Modulation			
Pace			
Strength			
Tone			
Articulation			
Personal mannerisms			

STANCE AND POSTURE	Good	Fair	Awful
Confidence			
Gestures			
Eye contact with the audience			
Personal appearance			
Use of the presentation area			

VISUAL AIDS	Good	Fair	Awful
Clarity			
Interest			
Number of slides			
Added value			
Equipment handling			

Chairperson's Introduction
Start time:
Finish time:

Presentation 1
Introduction time
Start time:
Finish time:
Summary time

Presentation 2
Introduction time
Start time:
Finish time:
Summary time

Presentation 3

CHAIRED PRESENTATIONS CHECKLIST	Good	Fair	Awful
Chairperson's intro			
Chairperson's links			
References from speakers to other presentations			
Chairperson's closing speech			
Overall links			
Logical order of presentations			
Handling of questions			

Templates

Groom's speech

■ Thank the bride's father for his toast and for giving you his daughter's hand in marriage.

■ Thank the bride's parents for organizing the wedding and for welcoming you into their family.

■ Talk of how happy this day makes you and how lucky you are to have such a lovely bride.

■ Praise your in-laws on having raised their daughter so well and show your positive feelings towards them.

■ Say something affectionate about your own parents.

■ Thank the guests for coming, for their good wishes and their generous gifts.

■ Thank the best man, ushers, the person who performed the ceremony and any helpers.

■ Propose a toast to the health and happiness of the bridesmaids.

Father of the bride's speech

■ Welcome the groom's parents, other relations, friends and distinguished guests.

■ Thank particular people by name for their help.

■ Comment favourably on how lovely the bride looks, praise her past achievements and thank her for being part of the family.

■ Welcome the groom into the bride's family.

■ To end, offer sincere congratulations to the happy couple and wish them well for the future.

Best man's speech

■ You represent other members of the bridal party, so don't forget to thank the groom for his words about the bridesmaids.

■ Let everyone know how you and the groom first met and how you feel about being his best man.

■ Tell how you met the groom, or an anecdote from the past.

■ Say something funny at the groom's expense. Does he like to cook? Does he have a reputation for being tight with money? Is he obsessed with football?

■ Think about the groom's character, interests and career.

■ Tell an amusing anecdote about the groom.

■ Say why you're his best man, delve into your mutual past and recite an entertaining story.

■ Don't forget the bride. Always make a point of saying something nice about the bride.

■ Provide an insight into the bride and groom's relationship. What do they see in each other?

■ Pay a sincere tribute to the groom. Now say something nice about him to reassure the bride's family.

■ The final toast. The bride and groom. The bridesmaids.

Master of ceremonies template

MC opening speech

■ Welcome everyone in the audience. Mention any special guests (for example, 'Good evening, Your Royal Highness, Prime Minister, Ladies and Gentlemen ...'.

■ Briefly introduce yourself.

■ Remind the audience of why they are there and what the event will achieve.

■ Outline the agenda briefly.

■ Cover any logistics briefly (what time the event finishes, when and where lunch or coffee breaks will occur, whether there are any hand-outs and whether there will be time for questions).

■ Introduce the first speaker and the subject of the first presentation.

MC links: Handling question time

■ Summarize last speaker.

■ Introduce next speaker, linking the presentation to the last one.

MC closing speech

■ Handle question time for the last session.

■ Summarize final presentation.

- Summarize the conference.
- Thank the speakers and the audience.
- Call to action.
- Close the conference.

Templates for business project meetings

Project presentations: First project meeting

- Welcome, objectives for the meeting, logistics for the meeting.
- Introduction of project manager.
- Introduction of project sponsor.
- Introduction to project:
  - project statement;
  - project scope;
  - project budget;
  - project quality checks;
  - project time schedule.
- Introduction of project team:
  - allocation of sub-teams and roles within the project;
  - project methodology;
  - project documentation rules;
  - project office and contact information;
  - meetings schedule;
  - discussion and question-and-answer session;
  - closing statements.

All this should be documented for each team member.

Project update meetings

(Keep these as short as possible.)

- welcome, objectives for the meeting, logistics for the meeting;
- project manager's report (progress of the project overall);
- team leader's reports;
- any variations from the project plan;
- update the risk list;
- 'any problems' session;
- set tasks;
- schedule next meeting;
- close meeting.

Training sessions

■ Welcome.

■ Introduce the trainer.

■ Introduce the training room and the kit.

■ Objectives for the training course.

■ Attendees introduce themselves and state their objectives.

■ Agenda and logistics.

■ Any questions?

■ Introduce first module:

– what it contains;
  – where this is in the manual;
  – why they need to learn this;
  – run the module.

■ Check what they have learned.

■ Any questions.

■ Introduce the other modules and run them in the same way.

■ Close the course:
  – summary;
  – what they have learned;
  – how to reinforce the learning;
  – final test.

Company briefings

■ welcome;

■ speaker introduction;

■ objectives of the presentation;

■ agenda and logistics;

■ information session;

■ for each item:
  – why they need to know this;
  – what the information is;
  – an example;
  – a recap;

■ question-and-answer session;

■ close the meeting.

Business reports

- welcome;
- speaker introduction;
- objectives of the presentation;
- agenda and logistics;
- background information;
- information session;
- question-and-answer session;
- close:
  - summary;
  - call to action.

Scientific reports and technical presentations

- welcome;
- speaker introduction;
- objectives of the presentation;
- agenda and logistics;
- glossary of terms;
- background information, previous research;
- information session;
- question-and-answer session;
- close:
  - summary;
  - call to action.

Demonstrations

- welcome;
- speaker introduction;
- objectives for the presentation;
- agenda and logistics;
- introduction of demonstration;
- first sequence of demonstration:
  - background information (what comes before this activity);
  - tell, show, explain;
  - summarize;
  - link to next activity;

- repeat until all items (no more than seven at one time) are covered;
- general summary;
- question-and-answer session;
- close:
  - call to action;
  - contact details and details of help desk where necessary.

Team-building presentations

- welcome;
- speaker introduction;
- objectives for the presentation;
- agenda and logistics;
- introduction of all team members;
- activity for team bonding;
- information session;
- question-and-answer session;
- close:
  - summary;
  - call to action.

Conferences

- coffee served;
- Chairperson opens session;
- objectives, logistics, agenda;
- introduction of first speaker and subject;
- first speaker;
- Chairperson handles question-and-answer session;
- summary of first presentation;
- link to second speaker and second presentation.

After two presentations the Chairperson should summarize the second one and announce a coffee break. After the coffee break Chairperson recaps second presentation briefly and introduces the third speaker.

After the final speaker and question-and-answer session the Chairperson summarizes the conference, thanks the speakers and the audience, makes a call to action and closes the conference.

Sales presentations

- welcome to the customer;
- speaker introduction;
- objectives of the presentation;
- agenda and logistics;
- background information, showing that the speaker understands the concerns of the customer;
- information session, stressing the benefits of what the presenter is selling;
- demonstration;
- examples of satisfied customers;
- question-and-answer session;
- close:
  - summary;
  - call to action: ask for the sale.

Fire fighting presentations

- welcome;
- speaker introduction;
- objectives for the presentation;
- agenda and logistics;
- background information;
- the current situation;
- who is affected;
- how this will be corrected;
- what will be done to ensure it doesn't happen again;
- question-and-answer session;
- close:
  - summary;
  - call to action.

Thank-you speeches

- welcome;
- quick self-introduction;
- introduction to the person you are thanking;
- what they have done;

- why this was valuable;
- heartfelt thanks;
- hand over to the person being thanked for their response.

Giving bad news

- welcome and introduction;
- why you are giving this presentation;
- the bad news (straight from the hip);
- whom it affects;
- how it will affect them;
- what can be done by the company to mitigate the bad news;
- what can be done by the individuals in the audience to mitigate the bad news;
- what the next steps are expected to be;
- reassurance if possible;
- summarize as positively as possible;
- question-and-answer session;
- close and call to action.

Giving good news

- welcome and introduction;
- why you are giving this presentation;
- the good news (personalizing this to the members of the audience as far as possible);
- how to build on the good news;
- what the next steps are expected to be;
- summarize;
- question-and-answer session;
- close and call to action.

Hints and tips on preparing presentations

Presentation structure

The human brain works in (quite often) an extremely predictable way, so unless you are dealing with the stranger forms of human life (e.g. knife murderers, musical geniuses, your manager) it is worth making use of the brain's function to get your message across.

Summary of presentation structure

It takes three passes at an experience to assimilate that experience properly, remember it and be able to act on it.

■ No one can listen carefully if they are distracted by 1) new situations, 2) physical needs, 3) uncertainty (people need a framework within which to listen and understand what is being said), and it helps to know why they need to listen.

■ People need reinforcement of new information to make it stick.

■ People remember best if they can relate the new information to past experience.

■ Visual imagery is retained longer than verbal or intellectual facts.

So, if you structure your presentation with these factors in mind, you have a very good chance of being remembered. This is the golden recipe:

■ Tell them what you are about to do, and what's in it for them.

■ Tell them why they are there.

■ Tell them who else is there.

■ Tell them who you are.

■ Give them time to get used to the physical surroundings.

■ Allay any worries about timing, note taking, question asking, handouts etc.

■ Get them interested.

Only then can you start the meaty part of the presentation, which is to:

■ Tell them what they need to hear.

■ Tell them using vocabulary with which they are familiar.

■ Tell them using examples they can use when they pass that information on.

■ Tell them in a way that allows them to make 'pictures in their minds'.

■ Tell them in a structured way and with a logical flow.

So having passed on all this vital information in a way that allowed your audience to process it efficiently, all you need to do now is to 'reinforce retention' (this is the edge you will get over the competition).

■ Tell them what you have said – but this time in a way that drives the conclusions home.

- Tell them what they can do to make this information really work for them.
- Tell them the next steps to take to make their credibility/competence obvious.
- Give them a 'call to action' that will make them do something that makes them remember what *you* said.
- Leave them energized and positive.

Flip chart questions and answers

One month has 28 days, of the remaining 11 how many have 30 days?
Answer: 4 (April, June, September, November).

A woman gave a beggar 10 pence. The woman is the beggar's sister but the beggar is not the woman's brother. What is their relationship?
Answer: The beggar is the woman's sister.

Why can't a consultant living near London be buried West of Oxford?
Answer: Because the consultant is still living.

Do they have a Fourth of July in England?
Answer: Of course.

How can you throw a tennis ball with all your might and have it stop and come right back to you without it hitting a net, a wall or any other obstruction?
Answer: Throw it straight up into the air.

Two fathers and two sons shot three deer. Each took home one deer. How was that possible?
Answer: Grandfather, father and grandson.

Visualize four horizontal lines, one above the other, now visualize four vertical lines, each one cutting through the horizontal lines. How many squares did you form (do not use paper and pencil)?
Answer: Nine complete squares.

Six men drove over 150 miles in a car. The trip took two hours, yet no one in the car noticed that they had a flat tyre the whole time. How was this possible?
Answer: The flat tyre was in the boot.

You are sitting in a room with 12 friends – can any of them sit in a particular place in the room where it would be impossible for you to sit?
Answer: On your lap.

Seven cars were lined up in a dealer's showroom bumper to bumper. How many bumpers were actually touching each other?
Answer 12.

Index

acoustics 76, 80, 107
aiming 29,
  see also communication
alternatives to presentations
    186–93
audience 20–24, 25–37
  active listening 34
  assumptions 30
  body language 33
  cautionary tale 23
  checking understanding 126
  concerns during presentations
      20, 23
  energising the, 156
  expectations 11–19
  participation 157
  researching your audience 20–24
  thinking styles, 35–37
authority 100, 101
autocues 111, 112

behaviours 25–37
benefits 7, 62
  of a presentation 7
  vs facts and features 62
body language 33, 101–06
borders 67
  see also visuals

charisma 100
communication 28–35
controlling your audience 94,
    155–57

decoding 34
  see also communication
delivering the presentation
    135–40
demonstrations 141–54, 214
disasters 194, 195
discussion 167, 168
displacement activities 102, 104

encoding 29, 31
  see also communication
equipment 120–25, 196, 197
evaluation 206, 207
expectations 11–19
eye signals 104

facts, features and benefits 62
first impressions 135, 136
following up presentations
    183–85

greeting attendees 16–19
handshaking 16, 17, 18

hints and tips on presentations
    217, 218, 219
hyperlinks   70–73

interruptions   157, 168
interviews   158–67

lecterns   79
lighting   80
logistics   15

master of ceremonies   117–82
media   158–69
meeting and greeting ritual
    16–19
meetings   186–92
memory   38–45
microphones   107–12

nerves   98–100
numerical data   43

objectives   48–51
    demonstration objectives   144
    S.M.A.R.T. objectives   48
organising your information
    51–53

plosives   93, 97
presentations
    constituents of a good   16
    disasters   194, 195
    endings   55
    example of a good   9
    example of a pointless   8
    expense of   5
    ingredients   2
    keeping the pace going   139
    middle of   57
    objectives   9, 48
    recipe   1, 2
    rehearsals   113
    structure   55

technical presentations   141
timescales   59
titles   58
training modules   173
transition to question and answer
    session   127
presentation area   79
projects   49, 64, 212
prompt cards   63
proxemics   105

question and answer session
    126–134

rapport   105
receiving   29, 33
    see also communication
rehearsals   113–19
rehearsal checklist   115
researching audience's time needs
    36
responding.   29, 34
    see also communication

sales cycle   151
scripting   56–64
    MC script   29, 33
    structuring   47–53
    wordage and time   59
scriptwriting rules   64
seating   76–79
self assessment   3, 199
spot the liar   105
staging   76–81
stress   104
selecting your subject   47–53

technical presentations   141–142
teleconferencing   192, 193
templates   210
training   170–176
    training others   173
    training yourself   170

transmission   29, 37
   see also communication
typefaces   69

venues   115
visuals   65–75
  bad backgrounds   66
  brightness and afterimage   65
voice   82–97
  accents   86
  breathing   82–85
  control   86

exercises for phrasing   94, 95
mechanics of speech   191
pausing and stress   95
pitch   88
plosives   93, 97
posture and breathing exercise
  90
resonance   86
volume   87
warming up   103

Warner, Samantha   120